THE PARTITION OF INDIA

Causes and Responsibilities

PROBLEMS IN ASIAN CIVILIZATIONS

UNDER THE EDITORIAL DIRECTION OF THE COMMITTEE ON ORIENTAL
STUDIES, COLUMBIA UNIVERSITY

EDITORIAL COMMITTEE: *Wm. Theodore de Bary*, COLUMBIA UNIVERSITY •
Ainslie T. Embree, COLUMBIA UNIVERSITY • *John Meskill*, BARNARD COLLEGE
• *Johanna M. Menzel*, COLUMBIA UNIVERSITY • *Arthur Tiedemann*,
THE CITY COLLEGE OF NEW YORK

Other volumes in preparation

PROBLEMS IN ASIAN CIVILIZATIONS

THE PARTITION OF INDIA
Causes and Responsibilities

Edited with an introduction by

T. Walter Wallbank
UNIVERSITY OF SOUTHERN CALIFORNIA

D. C. HEATH AND COMPANY · BOSTON

137818

Library of Congress Catalog Card Number 66–26814

Copyright © 1966 by D. C. Heath and Company

BOSTON   ENGLEWOOD   CHICAGO   DALLAS   SAN FRANCISCO   ATLANTA

PRINTED IN THE UNITED STATES OF AMERICA

PRINTED JULY 1968

Table of Contents

Introduction

THE Plural Society, and its frequent consequence, Partition, has become one of the contemporary world's most grievous problems. A Plural Society has been defined as "a society comprising two or more elements or social orders which live side by side, yet without mingling, in one political unit."[1] The logic of history would seem to call for increasing cooperation and even for forms of integration between disparate political units, but the contemporary world presents disturbing evidence of a contrary tendency. Various societies and political units have been or are being torn apart by rival groups made antagonistic by their differences.

The problem of the Plural Society and the tragic results stemming from failure to compose ethnic and cultural differences are best seen in the case of the subcontinent of India. The Partition of the political unit created under British rule is one of the most significant events in twentieth-century Asian history. This division was followed by violent strife in which thousands of Muslims, Sikhs, and Hindus lost their lives. Partition also rent the natural strategic and economic unity enjoyed by undivided India. And between India and Pakistan it created a constantly smouldering fire of discord symbolized by the Kashmir issue.

Was this Partition necessary, could it have been avoided, and what or who was mainly responsible? An attempt to explore these questions should not only throw light on the history of the Indian subcontinent in recent times but should also prove helpful in understanding and assessing the situation in other Plural Societies where Partition has, or may, come about and where peoples are divided by reason of race, religion, and culture.

In the many centuries that mark Indian history from its earliest civilization in the Indus valley (2500 to 1500 B.C.) to the majesty and creativity of the Gupta Empire (fourth and fifth centuries A.D.), the subcontinent experienced numerous invasions. The intruders, however, were usually absorbed into the all-pervading system of Hinduism and found a place in the societal structure. The caste system played an important role in this process, with Hindu society divided horizontally into many caste layers, but with all the strata forming part of a relatively harmonious whole. There was, however, one group of invaders who were not absorbed into the social structure of Hindu India. The various Muslim peoples who entered India remained a distinct entity in the social and political fabric of Indian life.

Muslim Arabs invaded and captured the area of Sind in western India during the eighth century but failed to expand. Islamic invasion, from Afghanistan and Turkestan, began in earnest in the tenth century and by 1318 the Delhi Sultanate exercised at least nominal control of almost all of India. Following its collapse, India passed under the control of the Mughal dynasty in the sixteenth century. The Mughals, like most of the former Muslim rulers, were Turks. Their empire expanded throughout the sixteenth and seventeenth centuries, but following the death of Aurangzeb in 1707 it rapidly declined.

Out of the struggle for power that char-

[1] J. S. Furnivall, *Netherlands India*. Cambridge University Press, 1939, p. 446.

vii

acterized eighteenth-century Indian political life, the British, in the form of the East India Company, emerged as the dominant force. The first important interference in Indian politics was signalled by the battle of Plassey in 1757, which established the nominee of the East India Company on the throne of Bengal, and within a hundred years the British gained complete control of the whole subcontinent. The uprisings of 1857 in North India challenged British rule, but failed to reestablish Indian rule. The next five decades of imperial rule performed three important functions: the creation of political unity; the introduction of western ideas; and the first tentative beginnings of representative government.

As to the Hindus and Muslims, the former quickly responded to the western impact that brought new opportunities in business, the professions, and government service. The Muslims, however, appeared stunned by the reversal of their fortunes. For several decades after the Mutiny of 1857 they remained apathetic, falling behind the Hindus in the New India that was emerging.

In the latter part of the nineteenth century, as long as British imperial rule appeared firm and lasting, there were few serious communal clashes. This term "communal" has a special connotation in Indian affairs. It refers to groups that are set apart by reason mainly of language, religion, occupation, and historical origin. Communal rivalry, especially between Hindus and Muslims, has been a distinctive feature of the Indian scene.

This communalism is described and analyzed in the selections forming Part I: Two Ways of Life? The most important aspects of the problem are evaluated, such as Muslim memory of imperial rule, economic rivalry, and the antithesis in religious doctrines and social customs. The denial by Jawaharlal Nehru that any such antithesis actually existed is, in essence, the position taken all through the period by the Indian National Congress. Since this was the position accepted by the overwhelming majority of non-Muslims, as well as that group of Muslims known as "National Muslims" who supported the Congress, the opposing view that India was in fact "two nations" had to be stated very strenuously. This explains why the majority of the readings are concerned with asserting differences; within the Indian context itself there was a tendency to deny the differences by silence or simply by the kind of analysis made by Nehru. It is this attitude that is deplored in the two later readings by R. C. Majumdar and I. H. Qureshi, the former a Hindu and the latter a Muslim. Both argue that the refusal to face the facts of history explains the bitterness and hostility created by Partition.

The Indian scene from 1857 to 1914 was characterized by the expansion of modern communications and transportation, the growth and widening use of English as a lingua franca, the establishment of western education, and the rise of a professional and business middle class. These trends helped to stir a spirit of nationalism which was signalized by the founding of the National Congress in 1885. In theory a truly national and secular party, the Congress was actually much more a Hindu than a Muslim organization in its membership. A Hindu religious and ideational renaissance that tended to be anti-Muslim as well as anti-British, and which was closely tied in with the rise of political nationalism, alienated some Muslims. This reaction is seen in the crusade of Sir Syed Ahmad Khan (1817–1898) who successfully set about creating a counter Muslim Revival. As a result of his labors the Muslim community was aroused from its torpor, set about adopting western education, and became imbued with a spirit of nationalism. One consequence was the founding of the Moslem League in 1906.

Meanwhile Congress nationalism advanced, supported by a small body of eminent Muslim leaders including Mohammad Ali Jinnah. The main body of the nationalistic movement was moderate in outlook, but it included a radical fringe that began to resort to terrorism in the 1890's. In response, Britain in 1909 enacted the Morely-Minto reforms, giving Indians a limited role in the provincial and central legislatures. The most controversial feature of the new system of government was that it provided communal electorates for the Muslim community. By this feature the Muslims were guaranteed a certain number of seats in the new legislatures, and these representatives could be elected only by voters on the Muslim communal roll. The leaders of the Indian National Congress regarded this as an attempt to divide Muslims from Hindus.

During the First World War the nationalist aspirations of the Indian people grew rapidly, and at its close Mohandas K. Gandhi emerged as the unchallenged leader of a mass movement demanding substantial political reforms from the British government. For a brief period Muslims and Hindus, through the Lucknow Pact of 1916 which promised a continuation of communal electorates, joined in an alliance and common front demanding a greater measure of self-government. But this detente between the Muslim League and Congress was short lived. During the 1920's communal strife between Hindus and Muslims mounted. The antagonism became more evident from 1930 to 1934 when a series of Round Table Conferences were held in London to draft a new constitution for India. Gandhi's assertion that he alone, as the spokesman for the Congress, represented India was hotly contested at the second Conference by the League delegates.

Most authorities agree that the period from 1937 to 1942 was critical in the growth of Muslim nationalism and the idea of Partition. In 1937 a new government of India act granted responsible government to the eleven provinces; in six of these Congress enjoyed a clear majority, and in four the Muslim League had the same position. In those provinces governed by a Congress ministry, and where there were large Muslim minorities, Congress refused representation in the cabinets to any Muslim not a member of this party. The League also asserted that the Congress provincial ministries abused their power, and charged that there was discrimination against Muslims in education and in the public services.

It was during this period that the political situation in India was transformed. Jinnah emerged from obscurity to become the idol of the Muslim masses and the Muslim League grew in membership and prestige. Some form of Partition had first been bruited by the famous Muslim scholar and poet Sir Muhammad Iqbal, in 1930. In 1933 a group of Indian Muslim students at Cambridge University presented a more definite scheme for the creation of a new Muslim state in India and gave it the coined name of Pakistan. As the 1930's closed, the idea of Partition, or at least some form of loose federation of semi-autonomous units was increasingly discussed. The Muslim League convened in the spring of 1940 to hear its president declare that the Muslims "must have their homelands, their territory, and their state." Jinnah was now asserting that the Muslims were not a minority but a distinct nation.

While stressing the growing Muslim demand for a separate state, it should be noted that a group of Orthodox Muslim scholars were strenuous opponents of the idea of Partition. Their arguments are examined in the selection by Z. H. Faruqi.

With the involvement of India in the Second World War, the power of the League steadily grew, and Jinnah's determination to achieve Pakistan hardened. In the late fall of 1939 all the Congress ministries in the provinces resigned when their demand for immediate self-government was refused. With Japan at the frontiers of India in 1942, the British War Cabinet dispatched Sir Stafford Cripps to India to try to rally all parties for the war effort. If Congress would thus join, Britain pledged in effect independence after hostilities ceased; and in order to mollify Muslim fears, it was further pledged that any province, so minded, could remain out of the proposed Indian Union. It was also to be agreed that there could be no basic changes in the constitution until the war ended. This offer was turned down both by the League and Congress, for different reasons. The former refused to admit the right of any province to remain out of the Indian Union; the latter maintained that the right of nonaccession was not made strong enough.

There still remained a slim hope that both parties, engaged in a common war effort, might reduce their differences. Gandhi's was the decisive voice in Congress turning down the Cripps proposals. The Mahatma now demanded that Britain "Quit India" and on the refusal of Churchill's government, Congress initiated a civil disobedience movement. The Government responded by imprisoning most of the Congress leaders, including Gandhi and Nehru, until the war was almost over. During these years the League had no opposition, and Jinnah worked unceasingly to strengthen his demands for Pakistan.

In 1944 there was a significant exchange of views between Gandhi and Jinnah. In this correspondence, included in Part II, Gandhi refused to admit the validity of the two-nation theory; but he did acknowledge that India was "one family consisting of many members," so plebiscites should be held to determine what separate self-governing states should be established. Another principle advanced by Gandhi, and one that later caused much acrimony, was that independence should come first, then the League and Congress differences could be solved. To these principles, Jinnah gave a firm veto. He argued that in the sovereign Muslim state he envisaged there could be no surrender of power to any suggested central government. And for the first time he indicated the exact frontiers of the Pakistan he and the League had in mind.

Such in brief outline is the general history of the Hindu-Muslim communal problem, together with British policy, from the Mutiny to the end of World War II. The second group of readings placed under the title "The Widening Communal Gap" presents various views on the course of history during this period. The first is an interpretation by Sir Theodore Morison of the Muslim Revival and the rise of political consciousness among Muslims. The next selection by Sir Hugh MacPherson surveys the history of communal antagonism. Both these authors were British civil servants in India and espouse what might be termed a pro-Muslim viewpoint.

In 1918, preparatory to the drafting of a new scheme of Indian government, the British Secretary of State for India aided by the then Governor-General surveyed the Indian political scene. In the famous Montagu-Chelmsford *Report* they evaluated the controversial communal electorates and gave the reluctant judgment that they should be retained. Again in 1930, the so-called Simon Commission presented a *Report* analyzing the state of politics in India. It maintained that Britain's only purpose was to act as a buffer and remain neutral in this antagonism. Separate electorates were defended and it was denied that they were a basic cause of communal trouble. Rather, the one single factor was considered to be the growing struggle for political power as Britain gave evidence of her ultimate aim of abdicating imperial authority.

Many sympathizers of Indian nationalism and its cause for freedom before World War II saw only the deft hand of British imperialism in Hindu-Muslim tension. Jabez T. Sunderland in "Hindu-Muslim Antagonism" asserted that Britain overexaggerated communal tension, and that if Muslims and Hindus were only left alone there would be no trouble. This champion of Indian independence wrote that before the British came to India there was no hostility and that British policy from the outset had been to foment division.

The most forthright and comprehensive statement on the Hindu-Muslim problem is to be found in the writings of Jawaharlal Nehru. Nehru takes the position that the

Muslim invaders were assimilated — that they became Indianized. There is, therefore, no such thing as a Muslim nation or even Muslim culture in India. The system of separate electorates is castigated as a British device for keeping power. Nehru quotes an excerpt from the British Montagu-Chelmsford *Report* which should be checked against the somewhat fuller extract given on pages 31–32.

One explanation that was given for the growing antagonism between the Indian National Congress and the Muslim League was that the Congress was, in effect, anti-democratic and authoritarian, obsessed by the idea that it alone could govern India and that no other party could speak for real Indian interests. It was this attitude, it is argued, that led the Congress after the provincial elections of 1937 to refuse to form coalition governments with the Muslim League and, in addition, for the Congress Party to control the provincial ministries. This case against the Congress is made in the selection from Sir Reginald Coupland, who argues that the Congress exhibited a "totalitarian mentality" and was determined to establish a one-party government. In his view the attempt to coerce the Muslim League failed and the reaction of Jinnah and his followers constituted "an historic turning point in the course of Indian politics."

Britain, weary of her imperial burden and exhausted from the world conflict, quickly made plain her intention of granting independence to India. Mr. Attlee's Labour Government made a declaration to this effect by the end of 1945, and in February Attlee announced the appointment of a Cabinet Mission to be sent to India where it would assist Indian leaders to draw up a new constitution for a free nation.

The Cabinet Mission arrived on March 24th and continued its labors for three months. Early in May a conference was held with the various Indian leaders in which the Congress representatives insisted that (1) any new constitution should provide for a strong central government; (2) British authority should be ended immediately; (3) a Constituent Assembly should have full and unfettered power to frame a new government. These conditions were vetoed by Jinnah. On May 16th the Cabinet Mission announced its own plan. Any notion of Pakistan was ruled out. A new government should be formed that provided for autonomous provinces, and limited specific powers should be exercised by the central government in a Union of India. In addition to this long-range plan there was to be an interim government, a short-term plan, in which the British Viceroy should be guided by an Executive Council in which all members would be Indian. During the last week of June 1946 there was hope of success as both the League and the Congress signified their intention of accepting the long-range plan. But hopes were dashed during the middle of July by Jinnah's repudiation of the long-range plan. August 16th was declared by the Muslim League as Direction Action Day. Demonstrations were to be called against both Britain and the League. The result was many disorders, including the terrible Calcutta riots.

Meanwhile, in September 1946, the Interim Government was set up with Nehru at its head. League representatives later joined, but members of the Executive Council continued their controversies. Time was now running out and civil war seemed to be a possibility. Prime Minister Attlee in February 1947 announced that the transference of power "to responsible Indian hands" would take place no later than June 1948. The Viceroy, Lord Wavell, was recalled in March and Lord Mountbatten appointed in his place. Events moved swiftly. On June 3rd the Viceroy announced the plan for Partition agreed upon by the Muslim League and the Congress. The British Government was eager to surrender its responsibilities as quickly as possible. On July 4th, 1947, the Indian Independence Bill was introduced into Parliament and quickly passed. Independence for two new Dominions, members of the Commonwealth, became a reality on August 15th.

The events from 1945 to 1947 have been the subject of much conjecture and debate. In the third part of this volume, "The Final Rupture," the Cabinet Plan is discussed and the significance of its failure evaluated. Maulana Azad insists that the Plan was practicable. He attributes its failure mainly to an irresponsible speech made by Nehru. In his discussion of these negotiations, Brecher describes Nehru's ill-timed statements but argues that neither party ever really accepted the Plan. And even if it had been adopted, Partition still could not have been ruled out because it "would have led to endless friction." Penderel Moon pays tribute to Britain's desire to maintain Indian unity. Agreeing with both Azad and Brecher, he refers to Nehru's unfortunate remarks but avers that before this event Gandhi had also "intervened with . . . disastrous effect." To Moon it was this earlier event that made Pakistan inevitable. Moon concurs with Brecher that such actions as Gandhi's and Nehru's — and Jinnah's in striving to make the Interim Executive Council unworkable — were the surface manifestations of deep irreconcilable League and Congress differences. The views of Sir Syed Ahmad Khan are recalled. Years before he had foreseen that "two nations — Muslim and Hindu — could not sit on the same throne."

Anything approaching finality in explaining the bifurcation of India must wait until the passage of time affords better perspective and also provides additional evidence, now hidden in various archives or concealed in the memory of individuals. The final group of selections, "In Retrospect," presents various views as held about a decade after Partition. An English journalist, Mosley, offers some views on the motivation of Jinnah; and most provocative are the arguments given by Maulana Azad who insists that Partition should have been postponed and that division was not inevitable. Professor Brecher examines the probable reasons why Nehru finally decided to accept Partition. Penderel Moon goes back to the initial seeds of serious distrust as they germinated in the 1920's. He emphasizes the role played by Gandhi who, apparently unconsciously, increasingly convinced Muslims that the Congress was a Hindu body. V. P. Menon would seem to place the most blame for division upon Britain and Jinnah.

In arriving at some basic conclusions regarding the forces, events, and personalities that influenced Partition, an attempt to weigh the following questions would seem relevant:

(1) Did Gandhi transform Indian nationalism into a Hindu-oriented movement that justifiably alienated Muslims?

(2) Did Britain introduce separate electorates as part of a larger policy of Divide and Rule?

(3) Was Nehru too secular and deterministic economically to respect and appreciate Muslim fears and religious sensitivities?

(4) Was it a tragic blunder for Jinnah to demand Pakistan in 1940 so unequivocally when his motive — as some believe — was mainly to use it as a bargaining counter?

(5) Were Muslim apprehensions directed against Congress policy from 1937 to 1939 justified?

(6) In retrospect, in terms of the course of history from the intrusion of the Muslim conquerors, could there be said to be a predisposition toward Pakistan should the appropriate conditions arise? Could it also be said that there was a possibility of averting this potentiality up to 1942; but was Partition inevitable after this date?

[NOTE: For reasons of space, footnotes have been omitted from the selections.]

The Conflict of Opinion

"It is necessary first to realize that the Muslim community exists and . . . that it is essentially different in texture and outlook from the Hindu community."

— PERCIVAL SPEAR

"The Hindu-Muslim antagonism in its modern form has nothing to do with race, and very little to do with the tenets of religion. . . . The real basis is economic and social."

— G. T. GARRATT

"It is a general Islamic dogma that Muslims should be governed only by Muslims, but Hinduism has no such religious criterion of rulership. The Muslim theory . . . leads to a view of the state as a theocracy . . . which makes Islam less a state religion than a religious state."

— W. NORMAN BROWN

"This idea of a Muslim nation is the figment of a few imaginations only, and, but for the publicity given it by the press, few people would have heard of it. And, even if many people believe in it, it would still vanish at the touch of reality."

— JAWAHARLAL NEHRU

"The true cause (of Hindu-Muslim tension) is the struggle for political power and for the opportunities which political power confers."

— SIMON COMMISSION

"There is absolutely nothing fundamentally antagonistic between the Hindus and Mohammedans of India. They have lived together for more than seven hundred years and are living together happily now, in essentially every respect except as stirred to rivalries, jealousies and temporary hostilities by the presence and plannings of a foreign government, whose constant policy is that of the old Romans, *divide et impera*."

— JABEZ T. SUNDERLAND

"The differences which separate Hindu and Muslim are essentially religious. . . . Purely religious causes explain most of the communal disturbances of which we have record. . . . It may indeed be claimed with justice that (Hindus and Muslims) have been drawn together, not severed by their century and a half under a common administration, which has given them the same laws, . . . the same progressive civilization and the bond of a common speech."

— HUGH MACPHERSON

"Gandhi slammed the door of negotiations in the face of Jinnah. . . . Jinnah now fully realized that the Muslims, as a separate community, had no political prospects in India. They had no chance of sharing political power with the Hindus; they must either surrender their individuality or cut themselves adrift from the Hindus."

— R. C. Majumdar

"(Some orthodox Muslim leaders) were convinced that the western-educated League leadership was exploiting the fair name of Islam for the worldly gain of Muslim vested interests which, knowing full well that the ignorant, Muslim masses could only be won over by appealing to their religious emotions, had given the signal that in a united India Islam would be in danger."

— Z. H. Faruqi

"More than anything else, there has been no sense of a common history; instead there are two views of such historical happenings as are capable of creating any emotion. . . . The attitude of the Muslim community toward the idea of Pakistan was, therefore, the logical consequence of its history."

— I. H. Qureshi

I. TWO WAYS OF LIFE

The Muslim Way of Life

PERCIVAL SPEAR

In the following selection Percival Spear analyzes the dichotomies between the Hindu and the Muslim way of life. While discounting race as a
crucial factor of differentiation, he does emphasize the basic incompatibility
between the two great Indian communities, which are poles apart in ways of
culture and sense of values. This incompatibility springs from the fact that
Islam and Hinduism represent a basic antithesis in practically all facets of life.
Spear, a Fellow of Selwyn College, Cambridge, for twenty-eight years was on
the faculty of Delhi University, and is the author of such scholarly works as
Twilight of the Mughuls and India: A Modern History.

GIBBON defined the Muslim creed as
a great truth and a necessary false-
hood. The student of politics in India
might call it a great fact and a necessary
division. It is necessary first to realize that
the Muslim community exists and has an
independent existence, and then that it is
essentially different in texture and outlook
from the Hindu community. Muslims are
not mere exceptions here and there to the
general rule of Hinduism; they are a large
and compact body of people who exist in
their own right and have to be considered
independently of the Hindus. They are not
simply people of different religious denomi-
nation, as Methodists might differ from
Roman Catholics; they are not people who
go to different churches yet have a common
culture and the same national outlook.
They are sufficiently different to consider
themselves a separate nation; they differ
from the Hindus not only in belief, but also
in culture, traditions, and, above all, in
their sense of values. A Methodist may feel
at home with a Roman Catholic on almost
everything except theology and worship,
but a Muslim must make an effort to feel at
home with a Hindu on anything outside
business. Dress, customs, food, codes of
conduct, and ideals are all different, and it
is only when these have been successfully
relegated to the background that the average Muslim can be at ease with the average
Hindu.

Having said so much, we must beware
of going too far. Muslims should not be
denied the name of Indian. For there is one
thing, in spite of all their differences, which
they share — the Indian temperament and
love of the soil. The Muslim Bengali has
much the same temperament as his Hindu
neighbour, though their ideas and customs
differ radically. Similarly, Punjabi Hindus
share with Muslims the Punjabi tempera-

From Percival Spear, India, Pakistan and the West (London, 1949), pp. 76–91. Reprinted by permission of Oxford University Press.

1

ment, as is shown by such common tastes as love of sport and love of a fight. A European parallel may be suggested in the northern and southern Irishman, and perhaps still more in the southern Catholic and southern Protestant, where there is emphatic conscious difference in almost every respect, but an equally emphatic affinity of temperament. Another parallel is that of French and British Canadians. Here temperament as well as tastes and opinions differ, but there is an underlying consciousness of belonging to the new world, and a common pride in being Canadian. The point to be grasped is that while the Muslim is a different species of Indian from the Hindu, he is an Indian for all that. He may look outside for help, but he has no longing to go outside to live; he may look to Arabia for inspiration, but he prefers Hindustan for its expression. Geographical India is his home, India the scene of his hopes and fears.

The initial contrast with Hinduism which strikes the observer is one of definiteness. If Hinduism may be compared to a cloud with its vague outlines and uncertain amorphous composition, Islam may be likened to a water-tower with its sharply defined shape and its very definite contents. You become aware of Hinduism by its atmosphere; you can tell Islam by its definite attributes. You become damp in a cloud; you record the shape of the water-tower and measure the water which flows from it. You feel Hinduism; you catalogue Islam. Thus, one says of Hinduism that certain things are to be found within it, but none of these things in themselves can be called Hinduism *per se;* with Islam one can take certain characteristics and say without hesitation "This is Islam." These characteristics are, briefly, a Creed, a Book, and a Brotherhood. The creed is that of the Prophet — "There is no god but God and Mohammad is his prophet"; the book is the Koran, which contains both dogma and rule of life; and the Brotherhood is the equality of all Muslims before God and to each other. This first distinction shows at once why Islam and Muslims are commonly more easily understood by Westerners than are Hindus and Hinduism. Christianity also has a Creed, a Book, and a Brotherhood, and though the characteristics of each differ widely from those of Islam there is a common approach to life, a common way of looking at things, which makes the Westerner and the Muslim feel more akin. Muslims and Christians both accept the world and seek to make the best of it; they have a creed about it and rules for living in it. Hindus do not accept the world, but seek to escape from it; they have a creed which denies its existence and rules to get out of it. For Muslims and Christians life is a probation for the next world and therefore supremely important; for the Hindu it is "doing time" in illusion and therefore without ultimate significance.

The Muslims in India numbered 96 millions out of a total population of 388 millions, according to the census of 1941. There may be some reason for doubting the accuracy of the 1941 figures since the relation of numbers to Assembly seats caused great efforts to inflate totals, but as both sides were equally energetic, the proportion of Muslims to the whole is probably accurate enough. The strength of the Muslim community is not, however, in exact proportion to their numbers. Dispersion saps their strength and is indeed one of the fundamental causes of the communal problem. If the Muslims had been a compact body in a particular area, like Ulstermen in Northern Ireland, some sort of division would have been comparatively easy, as it was in Ireland. But in fact, apart from certain areas of strength, Muslims are scattered all over the sub-continent, generally as a small minority. Even in the majority areas the majorities are not always overwhelming.

There are two main bodies of Muslims and a number of smaller groups. The first compact body is in the north-west, which forms what may be called the main Pakistan country. This region covers the tribal area of Baluchistan, the province of Sind, the North-west Frontier, the Punjab as far as the Sutlej, and the state of Bahalwapur. Adjacent to it lies the disputed territory of Kashmir. Here dwell what may be called the fighting Muslims, people with martial traditions, physical vigour, and sometimes of foreign descent. The second area of concentration is Eastern Pakistan, comprising eastern Bengal and the plains of Assam, with its spiritual centre in Dacca. The people here differ racially in no way from their Hindu neighbours. Apart from these two areas, which now constitute Pakistan, there are a number of Muslim *enclaves* among the Hindu population. Thus in the north the great cities like Delhi, Agra and Lucknow have substantial Muslim elements, and there are patches of Muslim settlement like the Rohillas (Afghans by descent) in Oudh and the Syeds of Barha. In the south there are substantial groups in Hyderabad state, and down the west coast from Gujarat to Travancore, including Bombay. For the rest there is a sprinkling of Muslims everywhere, more marked in the country than in the towns.

It is usually assumed that the majority of Muslims represent the "conquerors of India" in past ages. In fact, this is not the case, and it is well to be clear at the outset that the great majority of Muslims in India are Indians of Indian descent. Nevertheless their origins are diverse, and some understanding of them helps in estimating the complexity both of their composition and of their relations with the Hindus. The first group comes, of course, from the invading armies from the north-west. The word "armies" is used advisedly, for the Muslim invasions were distinguished from some of the earlier ones by the fact that they were not folk migrations, like the Teutonic and later Slav movements in Europe. They were the forays of raiding parties or the invasions of regular armies, and, as such, except perhaps in the north-west, they did not make large-scale settlements on the land. From the beginning these men formed a military and political governing caste, and though their numbers were big enough to form communities, they were professional and, so, scattered groups rather than agricultural and compact bodies. These men and their descendants formed first a military aristocracy, then a ruling class, and finally a social élite. Their traces can be seen to-day in the best Muslim families. It is a distinction, for example, to be a Qureishi, or member of the Arab tribe of the prophet Mohammad, a Syed or direct descendant of the Prophet, a Moghul or descendant of the northern adventurers of the sixteenth century, a Chagatai Turk, or an Afghan. The name Bokhari is an honoured surname, because it implies descent from the Turks of Bokhara in central Asia. This point is emphasized by the eagerness of aspiring families to annex an ancient patronymic. But when we have got so far, we have only accounted for a proportion of the ninety-six millions. In fact, the majority are of Hindu descent. Some of these are no doubt the result of forcible conversions. Periods occurred when this was done on a considerable scale, but in general it was a sporadic process resorted to in times of excitement such as the capture of a city and the looting of towns in the first flush of victory. Taken as a whole, Indian history has been remarkable for the clemency extended to the vanquished in war and for the regard shown to women and children. Amongst the many exceptions which prove the general rule, Timur's execution of 100,000 Hindu captives in a moment of panic before Delhi in 1398 may be matched by the record of raiding Marathas in the eighteenth century and of the Brigand Pindaris in the early years of the nineteenth. Owing to the ceremonial peculiarities of Hinduism, forcible conversion was curiously easy. Bring a Brahmin into contact with beef, for example, and he felt himself to be forever cut off from his kind; the profession of Islam was then the only, and by no means intolerable, alternative to joining the ranks of the outcastes.

In fact, however, the majority of conversions were of two kinds, individual among the upper-class Hindus, and mass among the lower. Many individuals among the upper classes have embraced Islam through the centuries, and some old-established Muslim families retain their Hindu names in pride of their Brahmin descent. Some changed their faith from conviction and others from policy; a list could be made of high Muslim ministers who were Hindu converts. Office was often worth a mosque, as Paris was once worth a mass. But the bulk supply, as it were, came from two main sources. All over India, but specially where the Muslims were firmly established in power or in considerable numbers, this creed attracted the Hindu outcaste. Its promise of brotherhood, its simple and concrete demands, its comparatively few taboos, opened up a new world to any outcaste who could see beyond the mud walls of his village; and it is perhaps only the rural isolation of India as a whole, together with the absence of effective Muslim power in large areas, which has prevented the absorption by Islam of the whole outcaste community. In eastern India another factor was at work. Bengal was the last resort of a popular if decayed Buddhism. Not long before the Muslim conquest the Buddhist was replaced by a militant Hindu dynasty, the traditional opponents of Buddhism. Thus, conditions resembled those in the Middle East before the appearance of Mohammad, and the Buddhists were inclined to welcome the Muslims as deliverers, as heretical Christians welcomed the Arabs in the seventh century. Not force but a release from tension made a Muslim of the eastern Bengali. There is one more factor, that of peaceful penetration along the west coast of India. Arab traders had their settlements from the discovery of the working of the monsoons in the first century and in due course became Muslims. These settlements multiplied by intermarriage and became indigenous Muslim communities in a predominantly Hindu country.

The nature of Hinduism made it necessary to describe the customs first and to infer from them the underlying ideas; the nature of Islam makes it simple to define ideas and beliefs first and consider the customs afterwards. What then must a man do to be a Muslim? He must first repeat the Muslim creed "There is no god but God and Mohammad is his prophet," and he should submit to the rite of circumcision. These are the two hallmarks of Islam. Belief in Mohammad means acceptance of his mission and so of his teaching which is enshrined in the Koran, and this involves certain theological, moral, and personal consequences. These are to be found in the three great systems of Muslim doctrine, Muslim morality, and Muslim law.

The essence of Muslim doctrine is the unity and transcendence of God. The unity of God makes the Trinity highly suspect if not incomprehensible to the Muslim, and the multiple gods of the popular Hindu pantheon positively repulsive. Its obverse side is the passionate rejection of idolatry, and though this may have been originally a Semitic characteristic, it is now thoroughly acclimatized in India. A temple is an idol house, dedicated to devils. Along with this goes an equal objection to the fertility aspect of popular Hinduism as specially manifested in the Siva cult. The transcendence of God involves an almost equally emphatic denial of the idea of divine incarnation. What in Christianity is the great exception which proves the rule of human frailty is endemic in Hinduism, so here is another great matter of difference. God, as the theologians would say, is completely "other" to the Muslim; he is high and lifted up, and who can attain unto him? The Hindu doctrine that God and the soul in man are identical is thus rank blasphemy to the Muslim.

From the creed we pass to the moral and ceremonial code. In many points the Muslim code resembles the Christian, for it has common origins. Mohammad borrowed heavily from the Jews, with whom he was in contact in Arabia. The Arabs in the great days of the Caliphate carried on the torch of Greek philosophy and imbibed the Aristotelean theory of justice. From these two systems many characteristics of Islamic law and practice derive and it is perhaps worth while to enumerate some of them briefly. The Jewish idea of fasting has found expression in the institution of the annual month of fasting called *Ramzan,* during which time no water or food may be taken from sunrise to sunset. As the Muslim calendar is lunar, this entails real hardship when the fast falls in the hot weather. The fast is still almost universally observed by Muslims in India. The Jewish Sabbath found its place in the Muslim observance of Friday as the day of congregational prayer. A visit to any large mosque on a Friday will demonstrate the abiding reality of this institution. From Judaism, also comes the Muslim idea of clean and unclean meats, particularly the prohibition of pork. The Judaic law is also influential in the personal law of Islam enshrined in the Traditions of the Prophet and the *Shariat.* To the Greeks, as one would expect, the Muslims are more indebted for ideas than for rules. Their ideas of God, of justice, of science are all influenced from this source. Muslim medicine is a direct carry-over from the Greek system, and to this day it is known as the *Yunani* or Greek system. Muslim mathematics continued where the Greeks left off.

But not everything Muslim is Greek or Jewish; Arabia has also its part in the Indian Muslim's heritage. The prohibition of spirits, genuine among the rank and file, but by no means universal among the upper classes, is of Arabian origin. So is the prohibition of music in worship, though it is popular enough in other respects. So also is the banishment of all representation of living forms from art, a decree which has proved effectual in sculpture and architecture if not altogether in painting. Islam has its sacred language of Arabic and its special ritual of prayer in the mosques. But the greatest of these Arab contributions has been in the matter of sexual morality. The Prophet himself allowed a limit of four wives, and perhaps because he himself overstepped the limit in later life, Islamic law recognizes the institution of concubinage or subordinate wives. In actual practice there is very little difference between Muslim and Hindu ruling princes and landed magnates in this respect, nor is there much in the lower and middle classes, for economic reasons. Plurality of wives is feasible only for the well-to-do who can afford their maintenance, and it can be said that among these the practice is declining because it is looked upon with increasing disfavour as being out of tune with the times. A second wife may be taken to remedy the lack of male heirs or under an infatuation when a man reaches "the dangerous age." But when all these "set-offs" have been allowed, there remains no doubt that the institution tends to undermine the position of Muslim womanhood. In many respects the Muslim woman is, on paper, freer than her Hindu sister. Marriage being a contract, not a sacrament, divorce exists and a woman may divorce a man as well as a man a woman. The woman as well as the man can also remarry. She has property rights distinct from her husband and a specified share in inheritance. A Muslim woman can be a person of substance in her own right. There are not wanting those amongst the poorer classes who exploit this institution of divorce by making a regular trade of decoying husbands and then decamping with the dowry. To get free the man must divorce the woman, who can then repeat the process. But this freedom for Muslim women is in India mainly on paper only. There can be little doubt that the position of the Hindu married woman is on the whole preferable so long as her husband is alive. This is due partly to theological considerations and partly to the institution of *purdah* or seclusion. Though the Hindu woman is not respected as a woman, she is significant in respects in which nearly all women share — as a sister, wife, and mother. She must worship her husband as a god, but she should be worshipped by her children as a goddess. The Muslim doctrine of women is much more severe. Without arguing the question of the female soul, it is clear that the woman is regarded as subordinate to, and mainly as a convenience of, man; and she is so frail, or such a temptation, that she must be kept apart from male society. She has no touch of divinity as with the Hindus. She cannot enter even the public part of a mosque to pray. The result of this is seen in the traditional failure to educate Muslim women, which means in turn that they cannot enjoy their large legal rights under Muslim law, firstly because they possess no independent means of livelihood.

The seclusion of women was not enjoined by Mohammad, nor is it practised in all Muslim countries. But it certainly exists in India and is too prominent a feature to be passed over. In the Punjab it is not practised in the villages except in the presence of total strangers, but it is an almost universal custom in the towns. The seclusion of women may be described as a social tunnel. The poorest classes have not the means, financial or material, to compass it; a step forward in the social march and it is a point of honour to enter the tunnel; at the furthest reach one emerges again into the light of general society. Seclusion and lack of education mean ill-health, ignorance, superstition, and apathy; education, on its side, is apt to mean revolt against seclusion. Tuberculosis is rampant among the secluded women of the towns, and affections[1] of the eyes are caused by the curious cotton grille in the white shroud which Muslim women should wear when in public, and through which they have to peer.

In social life the Muslim has his own dress and modes of address; if you cannot tell a Muslim by his clothes you can always rely on his mode of salutation. To some extent Muslim court dress and court manners spread all over India, as the influence of Versailles radiated all over Europe, but modern Hindus tend to substitute European manners and ceremonial dress, so making the distinction easier. The Muslim loves sport of every kind, from big-

[1] Infections [Ed. note].

game shooting to cock-fighting, pigeon-training, and kite-flying. He is a social being and lover of the good things of life. He delights in feasts and loves poetry, which he cultivates in poetical assemblies where rival poets declaim variations on set themes. Many men will quote the Persian poets or voice classical Urdu songs on the slightest provocation; it is as if London taxi-drivers drove the streets with Elizabethan lyrics on their lips. His religion is mainly a matter of outward observance, but in this he is punctilious. Often on weekdays, usually on Fridays and always on great days, the serried ranks of white-robed worshippers may be seen prostrating themselves in unison. The creed and the ceremonial emphasize the brotherhood; the brotherhood and the customs both promote unity and mark off the Muslims from the rest of the world. The Muslim as a believer in the one God has a unity of spirit with his fellows unknown to the Hindu, and it is this above all which has prevented his absorption by the Hindu sponge.

With over seven centuries of contact and conflict it would seem inevitable that the two systems must influence each other. In fact, their wide differences have made their mutual influence much less than might have been expected; the principle of repulsion has been more obviously at work than that of attraction. The Muslim influence has been mainly theological and the Hindu mainly social, each being most effective where its expression is most vigorous. The unity and moral character of God has been the side of Islam which has impressed the Hindu, and it has stimulated a series of reform movements prompted by the idea of mutual comprehension. All these movements, of which Sikhism is the largest, emphasize the unity of God and his demands on man, and all their leaders — of whom perhaps Kabir, the Muslim weaver of Benares, was the most eloquent — enjoin worship and moral practice above ritual or social custom. Most of these movements (again including Sikhism) condemn idolatry. On the Muslim side, Hindu pantheistic philosophy with its neglect of forms and distrust of the material, its tendency to identify God and Nature, its disregard of moral distinctions, has largely influenced the Muslim mystics or Sufis. In the sphere of religious practice a notable borrowing has been the habit of reverencing saints and, indeed, the dead generally. Lights are burnt, flowers are offered, as if at a Hindu shrine, and this tends to happen not only to recognized "saints," but to kings or anyone else whose tombs happen to come handy to the devotee. But perhaps the biggest loan from Hinduism is the practice of caste. It is true that Muslims in general would repudiate any such intention, and certainly the ideas behind caste are absent. But the idea of caste in its aspects of marriage restriction undoubtedly is to be found in the Muslim community. There are groups of Muslims who are almost as exclusive as separate castes, and in the lower classes are found many borrowings from Hindu customs which often are a mere continuation from Hindu times. But there is always the difference, perhaps vital, that such customs have social but not religious sanction, that their breach does not exclude from the Muslim brotherhood, and that all are united before God and in a crisis.

What are the things which keep Muslims and Hindus apart, which make them feel that they are different races and nations, which keep them permanently potentially on edge with each other? The first perhaps is the doctrinal issue of idolatry. The Muslim has borrowed from the Semitic races both his passionate rejection of polytheism and his passionate hatred of idolatry. A Muslim has not only an opinion about idolatry, but a deep-seated feeling, an instinct which affects his whole outlook on life. The worship of many gods, the portrayal of the divine in human form, is something to him which is less than human, the mark of the beast. It has, I think, no counterpart in the West; for it is far stronger than our ideas of good form or fair play or the behaviour of a gentleman.

The nearest analogy in Western experience is, perhaps, that of obscenity. The ramifications of these emotions are widespread through the whole realm of Hindu-Muslim relations because of the ubiquitous working of the Hindu doctrine of incarnation. So much in Hinduism is divine. The Muslim does not mind a Hindu not eating beef, for example, but he does object to his worshipping the cow. In times of irritation there is consequently a strong urge to kill a cow out of sheer bravado.

On the side of social custom the chief irritant among Muslims is the caste system in general and the claims of the Brahmins in particular. These claims offend the strong Muslim sense of equality and repel by their exclusiveness. The Muslim taboo of pork is another sore point in social relations, for though it is not a food of caste Hindus any more than of Muslims, its defiling effect makes it an easy subject for provocation. So, too, does the Muslim prohibition of music in worship. Pork in the mosque or music outside are certain ways of provoking a Hindu-Muslim riot.

But the mental anguish of mutual relations is not all on the Muslim side. Hindus suffer acutely in the ceremonial sphere. Hindu feelings about the cow are as untranslatable into Western terms as are Muslim feelings about idolatry, and they are no less strong. A Hindu may literally turn sick at the sight or smell of beef. Muslim practice in the matter of food seems to the typical Hindu to be impure, dirty, and degraded, something beneath the level of man. He cannot understand, on the other hand, what he calls Muslim fanaticism on the subject of idolatry. Orthodox Hindu and Muslim individuals can be, and often are, very good friends, but they usually take good care that their intercourse avoids these danger areas. The mined waters of the Indian social ocean are numerous and intricate and by no means clearly buoyed, and it is no wonder that not only the oblivious European, but sometimes Indians themselves, suffer sudden shipwreck therein.

These are some of the abiding sources of Hindu-Muslim misunderstanding, which are inherent in the two systems. To these must be added two subsidiary factors which happen to be potent today. The first is economic rivalry. The Hindu is a financier and business man, the Muslim in general an agriculturalist and soldier. So it happens that the Muslim is frequently in debt to the Hindu and has something of the feeling of the agricultural Arab towards the Zionist Jew in Palestine. The Hindu is the man who "does" him. This issue was vital in the matter of industrialization, since most of the industrial resources and nearly all the capital and skill of united India were in the hands of the Hindus. To the Muslim an industrialized India meant a Hindu India. Finally, there was the political issue. The Muslim had memories of empire and fears of servitude; the Hindus had the reverse. To the Muslim, Hindu rule meant Hinduization, or the break up of all that he held dear and the degradation of his most cherished values. It was therefore not surprising that when the Hindu stretched out his hand for the sceptre the Muslim cried out for Pakistan.

Economic Realities

G. T. GARRATT

Is Hindu-Muslim antipathy religious and racial? The author of this excerpt underlines the many points of similarity and cultural assimilation between the two communities and brusquely dismisses the importance of race and creed. He asserts that religious differences are utilized and exploited to camouflage and advance political and economic interests. In short, communal rivalry is really economic — the desire for material gain and for political jobs. G. T. Garratt (1888–1942) was a prolific writer on Indian subjects in the 1930's, after having served for ten years in the Indian Civil Service. He was the co-author, with Edward Thompson, of *Rise and Fulfilment of British Rule in India* and the editor of the well-known work *The Legacy of India*.

THE division between Hindus and Moslems is only one of these many vertical cleavages in Indian society. It is, however, far the greatest. The quarrel between the two religious groups has become a severe disease of the body politic. It needs to be analysed in the cool and dispassionate way in which scientists approach the similar problem of cancer. Nothing must be taken for granted, and the first point which needs examining is whether it is, as usually assumed, a religious and racial question. There has been a tendency to accept too readily the romantic idea of the Indian Moslem as a stranger keeping his desert faith pure in a land of idolaters. This view has been endorsed, not unnaturally, by the upper-class Mohammedans themselves. It is intensely gratifying to the educated Moslem, as he watches his people being ousted from power and place by the subtler Hindu, to consider himself, in the words of one of their leaders, as "a member of a universal religious brotherhood, sojourning in a land in which a neutral government, with a neutral outlook, kept law and order and justice." It is equally pleasing to the self-esteem of the impoverished Mohammedans, who make up such a large proportion of the *bazar* population of the small towns, to feel that they have some vague connection with the great world outside. They like to think of their co-religionists in Persia, Turkey, and Egypt enjoying an independence and freedom unknown to the Hindu, and especially to that fat and prosperous Hindu who happens to be living next door. The world is full of groups, like the "poor whites" of South Africa, relying on their connection with some dominant race elsewhere. The claim is natural enough, but the English, in accepting this picture of the Moslems as a race apart, seem to have been misled by a writer of genius, who had, however, a journalist's flair for the picturesque. . . .

The investigations of census officers make it clear that the vast majority of the Mohammedans in India are the descendants of converts from Hinduism. Fifteen per cent is a very generous estimate of the Punjab Moslems who are really of foreign

From G. T. Garratt, *An Indian Commentary* (London, n.d.), pp. 172–179. Reprinted by permission of Jonathan Cape Ltd.

9

origin, and in the rest of India — except the extreme North-West — the proportion of foreign stock is insignificant. As the Punjab contains only a fifth of India's 69 million Mohammedans, it is not unfair to consider those of foreign origin as a small and select aristocracy not incomparable with the old British stock in the United States of America. The remainder are only separated by a few generations from the various Hindu castes from which they were originally converted. Nor have they become, to any great extent, a mixed race, for the old caste distinctions have survived amongst these converted Hindus, just as they have amongst the Southern Indians who have been converted to Christianity. The castes hardly intermarry, and sometimes will not even inter-dine.

Although the distinction between section and section is much looser than in the case of the Hindu castes, and it is the fashion to deny the existence of rigid partitions between the various groups, yet there is practical endogamy in the sectional and functional divisions, and in Bengal a Sheikh will not marry a Kulu, while in some parts one Mohammedan will not feed with another. . . .

The racial distinction of the Moslems is clearly an illusion. They are in no sense foreigners, and Hindu blood runs in the veins even of the Mohammedan aristocracy. Six of the Mogul Emperors, including Jahangir and Shah Jehan, had Hindu mothers, and in the seventeenth century this form of intermarriage seems to have been common. The great mass of middle- and lower-class Moslems are only a few generations removed from their Hindu kinsmen. There are many races in India, well-differentiated stocks of great antiquity, Pathans, Parsis, Marathas, Telugus, Bengalis and Burmans, but it is only in a few parts of Northern India that two different races are brought into contact with each other, and that one of these is Hindu by religion and the other Mohammedan.

The nature of the two religions is such that it is often said to divide the Moslems clearly and irrevocably from the Hindus. At first sight this would appear to be true. Hinduism is the religion of the forest, Mohammedanism that of the desert. The beauty of Hinduism lies in the virtues of submission and dependence, its weakness lies in ignoring the will, its failure in the merging of the individual into a class, so that class consciousness becomes a substitute for conscience and will. It is the religion of men overwhelmed by nature, whose myriad gods swarm in the tree-tops. It tends to inaction, to sitting "by the Jumna's bank, waiting and musing and longing to die." Such a religion could never have survived in the desert, where a man is thrown upon his own resources, where independence is the cardinal virtue, and where a man inclines to a simple philosophy and a direct approach to the Deity. The fundamental incompatibility of the two creeds has undoubtedly tended to estrange Hindu and Moslem, and has to some extent thrown the latter on the side of the "other people of the Book," the British, but it is easy to exaggerate both tendencies.

The pervasiveness of Hinduism has already been discussed, and the desert religion has undoubtedly been modified by contact with it. Many Mohammedan communities retain caste, and also observe Hindu festivals and ceremonies. In some parts of the Deccan the Moslems seem not unlike a Hindu caste. They keep the Moharram, to which they invite certain Hindu castes, but they attend the Divali festivities. There is a famous shrine at Nagore which attracts both Hindus and Moslems, and in Gujerat and Sind there are many borderland sects, like the Matia, Momna, and Sanghar groups who base their creeds on both religions. Nearly every one with Hindu blood in his veins appears loath to break entirely with the Gods of the country. . . . In many districts the Moslems have modified the simplicity of their marriage ceremonies by introducing the *Shabgasht*, or night procession, and other Hindu rites. Even among the aristocratic Moslem families of Lucknow and Patna certain Hindu customs are found, and the remarriage of widows is uncommon.

Race is clearly not the basis of the Hindu-Moslem antagonism, and religion would seem to be only a partial reason for the continual outbreaks between the two communities. If the nature of the Moslem religion was the chief cause there would never be any peace in the land, and it would be difficult to explain why the hostility seems to come in waves, why it is much less common in Indian States than in British India, and why, until the Moplah rising, it was almost unknown in many parts of the south and west. Like the doctors in their investigations of cancer, one is driven to the conclusion that the germs of the trouble are nearly always present, but that they only become virulent when there is some other cause of irritation. When this becomes acute the other preliminaries to a quarrel are seldom lacking. The playing of music before mosques and the sacrificial slaughter of cows are little more than the formalities which precede a fracas between two groups "spoiling for a fight." . . .

A map, showing the areas where Hindu-Moslem outbreaks are most frequent, suggests that this added cause for irritation is really economic. The communities in these districts are divided into distinct economic groups. Thus, in the North-West, Hindus are the moneylenders and the Moslems are peasants; in the North-East they are often landowners and the Moslems tenants. In the towns, and it is in the towns where the feeling is worst, the shopkeepers, professional men, and employers are Hindu, the craftsmen and workers are usually Moslem. So much have the Hindus in the Punjab become identified with landowning and moneylending that the Land Alienation Act, aimed at assisting and protecting peasants of both religions, has now become the basis of a bitter quarrel between the two groups. The introduction of the machinery of democracy, and the insti-tution of the communal electorate have further confused religion and economics. Every politician knows that it is easier to arouse popular feeling upon a simple religious issue than upon a complicated social or economic question. The question of unemployment in England empties the House of Commons as quickly as a debate on the Prayer Book fills it. There is no cry in the world so effective as "The Church in danger," and in every Indian province, where a creed or a caste is in a minority, this cry is being raised. The educated classes, who employ it, have even less cause to divide upon religious questions than the masses. Many of the leading politicians have their full share of Western skepticism, and their European education has rounded off the angularities of the old creeds. It would be ridiculous to consider Mr. Jimnah and Mr. Jayakar as the rival protagonists of the religion of the desert and the religion of the forest. The Hindu-Moslem antagonism in its modern form has nothing to do with race, and very little to do with the tenets of religion. . . . the real basis is economic and social. Amongst the upper classes of India the fight is for the most part over offices and Government appointments. Amongst the working classes it takes different forms in town and country, and from province to province, but whether they appreciate the underlying forces or not, there are always priests and *moulvis,* newspapers and politicians to keep the latent irritation from dying down, and to spread through the *bazar* those rumours which breed fear and distrust. In many northern towns the situation closely resembles our ideas of mediaeval Italian cities, with the craftsmen-shopkeepers sitting at their work, but always ready to put up their shutters at the first sign of a faction fight. During a recent visit to India the writer came across two cases of serious rioting involving the closing of the *bazar.* The first arose from a quarrel between a Sikh soldier and a Moslem shoemaker who had sold him a bad pair of slippers. The second occurred because a Mohammedan boy had stolen a handful of sweets from a Hindu shopkeeper, and slipped and hurt himself when running away from the irate owner. Under-employment is rife in towns as well as villages, and there are always plenty of badmashes ready to join in a fight, especially if there are any prospects of loot.

Hindu-Muslim Differences

W. NORMAN BROWN

In the following selection, Professor W. Norman Brown of the University of Pennsylvania suggests that the communal problem has its roots in two profoundly different interpretations of man and his place in society. These fundamental attitudes color the whole of life, making it possible for Hindus and Muslims to give very different analyses of the social and political events in which they were both participating. Professor Brown also emphasizes the importance for later developments of the idea of the state held by the Muslims. In addition, he stresses the different nature of the impact of British rule on Hindus and Muslims, pointing out the important part this played in the growth of communalism.

Professor Brown is one of the most distinguished American authorities on Indian history and culture. His parents were missionaries and he spent his early years in the subcontinent. Receiving his doctorate in Sanskrit from Johns Hopkins in 1916 he returned to India as a professor in the Prince of Wales College in Jammu, Kashmir. Later he was appointed Professor of Sanskrit at the University of Pennsylvania.

THE basis of Hindu-Muslim communalism lies in cultural differences. Before partition these appeared to political leaders of the two communities in contrasting ways. The late Mohammad Ali Jinnah, head of the Muslim League, during the latter part of his career consistently said that the differences were not merely those of theology. Hinduism and Islam, he affirmed, were more than two different religions; rather, they were two different civilizations — so numerous and profound did he consider the antitheses — and, therefore, the two communities were more than a majority and a minority within a single India; they were two different nations which were incongruously associated under a single government. That had long been a Muslim position; it became the fundamental dogma in his political philosophy.

But non-Muslim political leaders took a different view. Jawaharlal Nehru, speaking for the Indian National Congress, in viewing the communal problem, said in his *Discovery of India* (1946), that the native Hinduism and the intrusive Islam had become only modifications of a common civilization. And Sir Tej Bahadur Sapru (1875–1950), a distinguished elder statesman of India, and a nonparty conference committee in its report on Constitutional Proposals (published in December 1945) took the same position. Jinnah emphasized the contradictions between the two communities; Nehru and Sir Tej Bahadur, the correspondences.

In these opposing views is illustrated the most fundamental of the Hindu-Muslim divergences. Islamic or Muslim civilization is centered around the religion of Islam,

Reprinted by permission of the publishers from W. Norman Brown, *The United States and India and Pakistan* (Cambridge, Mass.: Harvard University Press), pp. 130–140. Copyright, 1953, 1963 by the President and Fellows of Harvard College.

and one of the most characteristic features of that religion is the demand for doctrinal and cult uniformity. Only one view of God is acceptable, namely, as Allah; only one series of revelations concerning Him exists, namely, that of the prophets, of whom Muhammad is the last and the "seal"; only one book contains the divine message, the Koran; only one standard of duty lies open to man, submission to this revelation as a Muslim. But the religion of Hinduism, which is the core of native Hindu civilization, does not demand such uniformity, even as an ideal; rather it is latitudinarian and tolerant. With orthodox sanction and practice, Hinduism permits an unlimited variation in belief concerning the nature of God and a corresponding diversity in cult and standards of behavior.

Hinduism believes that mankind is incapable of achieving uniformity because human beings are inescapably affected by all their actions (*karma*) in previous existences, which give them at the instant of birth unequal endowments of intellect and spirit as well as unequal economic and social position, and therefore impose upon them different duties. Thus it sanctions the institution of caste, with its undemocratic implications. But orthodox Islam democratically views all mankind as born equal; it considers, in fact, that all infants are born Muslims; it is their misguided parents who turn them into Christians, Jews, Hindus, Buddhists, Sikhs, or others. Hinduism, therefore, logically recognizes different capabilities and prescribes different duties for the different castes. It is, from the Hindu point of view, unrealistic to expect human beings, so unequal in their capacities, to hold the same dogmas. Except in the case of the very rare souls who comprehend absolute truth, everyone is partly right and partly wrong, though in varying degrees.

What Hinduism demands is that, since difference of position, function, and duty exists as a fundamental feature of the cosmos, people of one persuasion should not interfere with people of another but leave them alone in their relative ignorance or wisdom and in the activities corresponding to their limitations. Proselytism is useless and troublesome; it may even be harmful. If an individual performs adequately the duties of his present state, he may in some future existence repair his present spiritual inadequacy and win nearer to supreme knowledge and truth. But Islam, with equally logical deductions from its premises, believes in missionary enterprise and the conversion of the infidel and the erring to the single revealed standard which it recognizes.

These contrasting attitudes are not without exceptions in their own communities. Many Muslims, especially today in the Near East, take a wider view of civilization and even of religion than strict and literal orthodoxy would admit; and there are some such too in India and Pakistan. So also there are in India many illiberal and overly dogmatic Hindus who are intolerant of sectarian belief other than their own and scornful of those outside their own narrow group. Yet the basic contrast remains generally true. Hence Islam makes a bifurcation of civilizations into the Islamic, which fundamentalist Muslims regard as God-inspired, and all other civilizations, which are by nature heterodox and false. But orthodox liberal Hinduism may easily admit all civilizations to be reconcilable as merely variations within a single great civilization. It is a corollary of the Muslim view to regard cultural multiplicity as a temporary evil to be replaced by the solitary existence of the one true culture and extinction of its rivals. Cultural amalgamation is equally a corollary of Hindu theory.

Related to this basic difference in outlook upon life is a difference in the social cohesiveness of Muslims and Hindus. With the high importance which Muslims attach to dogma and their generally democratic social order, they have developed a strong sense of community. This expresses itself to the eye in congregational worship in the mosque. There a great courtyard may be filled with a thousand faithful worshippers, whose voices and bodies rise and fall as one in the unison of prayer. Any similar phenomenon is unknown in Hinduism. When a Hindu goes to a temple, he worships alone and in undertones. Many temples have only recently been thrown open to all castes. Caste has, indeed, split the Hindu's society and intellectual freedom has individualized his religion. His human utopia is a state of philosophic anarchy; the Muslim's is the well-drilled regiment. The sense of membership in a community, despite sectarian differences, gave Islam the drive that carried it, within 110 years after the Hegira (A.D. 622), across North Africa and into Spain and France in the west and as far as the river Indus in the east. The Muslim consciousness of community has been strong in India, where the Muslims were a minority. There, in spite of sectarian theological and political differences, it gave them a power of aggressive action out of proportion to their numerical strength.

Again closely related to the fundamental contrast between Islam, with its unitary and dogmatic conception of life, and Hinduism, with its multiple and relative conception, is a difference concerning the relationship of the state and religion. It is a general Islamic dogma that Muslims should be governed only by Muslims, but Hinduism has no such religious criterion of rulership. The Muslim theory, in its orthodox and extreme form, leads to a view of the state as a theocracy (a term decried by Muslims in Pakistan because Islam has no priesthood), which makes Islam less a state religion than religious state. Muhammad regarded himself as the "warner" of his people, calling them to "submission" (islam); their duty was to become "submissive" (muslim) to Allah's will. The function of warner was considered a function of the state, to make conversions to the faith the state's highest purpose. That is why the Islamic religion has been promoted by military and political means as has no other. The law of the state is the Shariah

(shari'ah), that is, the manifested way, highway, divine law of God, sometimes defined as "that which would not be known had there not been a divine revelation." It is the duty of the divines to ascertain and interpret this and of the Islamic state to enforce it.

The early Muslims viewed the world as composed of two hostile military camps. One was the "abode of Islam" where the true faith was established; the other was the "abode of war" where Islam was not established and false doctrine prevailed. The ruler of the faithful was under obligation to convert the abode of war into the abode of Islam. This he might endeavor to do by making a demand of conversion upon the unbeliever state. If this were accepted, all was well; but if not, then he must wage a holy war (jihad) of compulsory conversion. The conquered were to be treated in two ways according to their previous religious condition. "People of the Book" — Jews, Christians, Magians, Sabaeans — whose scriptures precede the Koran and are considered by Muslims to be in the correct though incomplete line of revelation, had the choice of becoming Muslims or of accepting "protection" and paying a capitation tax. If they refused conversion, their lives were spared but they could not enjoy citizenship. People who were not of the Book had either to become Muslims or be put to death. Obviously, the harsh and extreme application of Muslim theory was impracticable where the conquered folk was stubborn yet necessary to supply labor for the true believing conquerors. For this reason conquered people, including many Hindus, were often allowed to keep their religion and their life, though it might be with impoverishment, humiliation, slavery.

Traditional Hindus have no such theory of the state. They do not regard it as divine will that all people should be Hindus under a single rule. To the traditionally educated Hindu the Muslim theory that state and religion are identical is illogical and untenable. When the Muslims overran

India and made forcible conversions, as they often did, the Brahman regarded the conquerors as, in this respect, irrational and mentally immature.

Other important cultural differences separate Hindus and Muslims. The Hindu prestige system, the institution of caste, wherein all men are born to graded places in society, with the Brahman on top as "a god on earth" and the Untouchable at the bottom deeply offends Muslims, since it relegates them, as it does all non-Hindus, to a low status. Islam is socially democratic. It teaches that all men, at least all Muslims, are equal. Again, Hindus decorate their temples profusely with images of gods, human beings, and animals, and use idols in worship as symbols to call a deity to mind. But the Koran strictly forbids the representation of any animate objects, and Muslims destroy the Hindus' temples and images, thus in Hindu eyes committing sacrilege. The Hindu attaches a peculiar sanctity to the cow and considers cow-killing only less heinous a sin than Brahman-killing; the Muslim regards the cow as legitimate food or sacrificial victim and when he can do so with impunity will not hesitate to slaughter the sacred animal. Hinduism uses the native Indian Sanskrit as its classical and sacred language and writes its books in native Indian scripts; Islam uses the imported Arabic and Persian languages and writes in the Perso-Arabic script. Hence the two, with only rare exceptions, have not read and cannot read each other's books. Muslims have generally felt it useless to understand the beliefs and social practices of the Hindus, and the Hindus have been prevented by traditional caste rules from marrying outside their endogamous groups or even interdining and so have been denied much social intercourse which would have helped to bring understanding and toleration.

Bitter and historic enmity divides the two faiths. The Hindus cannot forget the thousand years from the Arab invasion in 711 to the end of the emperor Aurangzeb's reign in 1707, when Muslims periodically plundered their homes, looted their cities, burnt their books, demolished their temples, slew their priests, abducted their women; and they fear a recurrence of these horrors if they should have to live again under Muslim power. With the Muslims it rankles that, under the pax Britannica, they came to take second place to the Hindus whom they had once vanquished and ruled.

Before the agitation that led to partition, in trade unions and peasant groups members of the two communities had often learned to work in cooperation. Among the ruling princes, the antipathy might be suppressed or ignored. It was the middle classes, economically ambitious, that were the chief field in which it appeared. They attached the most value to strict religious dogma; at the same time the system of communal legislative representation and political appointment produced in them heated rivalry and permanent tension, which they communicated on opportunity to the masses. Thereupon on some minor provocation, Muslim mullahs, Hindu priests, or fanatic laymen of either community might, by raising the Muslim cry of Din ("the Religion") or the Hindu charge of sacrilege, precipitate a riot.

Several aspects of Hindu-Muslim relations, which showed some degree of cultural assimilation, used to give proponents of the one-nation theory some ground for hope that at a future time, however remote, the hostility might disappear. The one which leaders of the Indian National Congress most often used to stress is the fact that Hindus and Muslims in each locality of India and Pakistan belong to the same racial and ethnic stock. Islam spread in India by conversion rather than by immigration. And conversions were made not so much by force, though force was often used and the memory is bitter in Hindus, as by missionary enterprise among the lowest in the Hindu social and economic scale, who found relief from many disabilities in accepting Islam. In every part of India and Pakistan Hindus and Muslims are alike physically; they can be distinguished only by externals, such as dress, treatment of facial and head hair, sectarian markings, customs of eating, drinking, or other. Moreover, in every locality both parts of the population use a common speech.

Socially, too, there has been occasional assimilation of the two groups, for example, in using similar wedding ceremonies and in sharing each other's religious festivals. Muslim dress has affected, though seldom completely supplanted, native Hindu middleclass costume. The Muslim habit of secluding women became a local practice of those Hindus who could afford it. Caste, though contrary to Muslim doctrine, nevertheless exists in a number of Muslim groups, which did not rid themselves of caste distinctions when accepting conversion.

On the intellectual level there exists a body of common material, as in the traditional mathematics, astrology, medicine. For several centuries, particularly during the sixteenth and seventeenth, Muslims translated Sanskrit works into Persian, which probably were not read much, yet showed a tendency toward community interrelationship. During that same period both communities had a certain amount of common vernacular literature. In architecture native Indian and imported Persian have blended to produce forms frequently employed in both Hindu and Muslim secular buildings, while in temple and mosque construction there has been exchange of many individual structural and decorative elements. Painting as practiced by both communities during the past three centuries has also been a fusion, in varying degrees in different localities, of native Indian and imported Persian.

Even in religion there have been approaches to each other. Muslim mysticism, that is, Sufiism, though unpalatable to Islamic orthodoxy, renders its adherents and Hindu mystics mutually intelligible. Compromise religions have been preached by persuasive teachers who drew ideas from both Hinduism and Islam. Kabir (1440–1518) was one, there are still sects bearing his name; another was Nanak (1469–

1538), the founder of Sikhism. The great Mughal emperor Akbar, who ruled from 1556 to 1605, tried unsuccessfully to bring Hindus and Muslims to a common type of worship, which he called Din Ilahi, but probably doomed it by naming himself God's vice-regent; it had only the merest handful of adherents and perished with him. Generally the reconcilers of the two faiths have done less in bringing them together than in creating new sects to complicate still further the varied array of India's religions.

Finally, the two communities have much of common history. Rulers of one faith have frequently made alliances with rulers of the other against rulers of their own faith. Muslim rulers have often used Hindus as civil administrators and generals, and Hindus have done the same with Muslims. During the British period in India the hereditary rulers of each group were deprived of their political power by the intruding Europeans, and the masses of both suffered economically as their agrarian system was revolutionized and their handicrafts put in competition with western machine industry. The two communities, on high and low levels alike, had a measure of joint interest in gaining self-rule.

The various religious and other cultural differences defined the two communities and produced their primary misunderstandings. But these might have been overlaid and become negligible in their effect upon national life if they had not been supplemented by economic disparities and political rivalries. It happened that in several large areas there was a religious dichotomy of landlords or moneylenders and peasantry. The one would be Muslim, the other Hindu. Thus, in the United Provinces (now Uttar Pradesh), where the peasantry was Hindu, there was a large class of Muslim landholders, called *taluqdars*. The reverse situation existed in parts of Bengal and the Punjab, where the Muslim peasantry paid rent to Hindu landlords or interest to Hindu moneylenders. In such situations, the clash between economic classes was sure to become identified with religious difference.

There was also rivalry between the Hindu and Muslim middle classes created in part by an accident of geography. Because the Muslims had entered India from the northwest and were chiefly concentrated in the north and away from the seaports where the British had entered and conducted most of their activities, it was the Hindus, living in and near those ports, who first profited economically from British commerce and first took advantage of the new western education. They became the agents to spread this education, and this fact, too, operated to the Muslim disadvantage and discontent. In Bengal Muslims avoided the learning which was brought by western unbelievers and propagated by Hindu idolaters. Further, when the British reorganized the system of land tenure, the new landlords under the British were Hindus, who had previously been only tax farmers under the Muslim regime. The old Muslim upper classes remained as landowners in their own areas, but the newly appointed Hindus became their upstart rivals as a prestige group and partly displaced them and reduced their numbers.

It was also the Hindus who developed the new bourgeoisie. By the time of the Indian Mutiny in 1857 the Muslim community had only a small middle class against the relatively large Hindu professional, clerical, and commercial groups. This condition persisted down to the time of partition. It was said that in East Bengal, now part of Pakistan, 80 per cent of trade and commerce was in Hindu hands. Moneylenders were almost all Hindus, and the jute business, which is the major industry of East Bengal, was also Hindu.

Similarly, about 90 percent of the professional classes were Hindu. This situation has altered under Pakistan. It was also the Hindus (and Parsis) who became the new industrialists, not the Muslims, most of whose leaders continued to be of the old landholder class.

There was another situation in the nineteenth century operating to Muslim disadvantage. When the Indian Mutiny occurred it was considered by the British to be a responsibility of the Muslims. Most of the Indian princes involved were Muslim, and the head of a freed India, as the Mutiny would have made it, was to be the titular Mughal emperor in Delhi, around whose shadowy figure the mutineers had assembled their forces. Because of this fact, the British, after quelling the Mutiny, laid the heavier part of the penalty upon the Muslims. It was approximately a decade later before they lifted this discrimination.

During the second half of the nineteenth century the Muslim community contained the larger part of India's dispossessed and unhappy great. It no longer had the political supremacy enjoyed under the Mughals, whose might had been destroyed by the Hindu Marathas and the Christian British, both of them infidels. The greater number of government posts open to Indians fell to Hindus, and the profits of business were theirs as well. By the time the century was three-quarters past, the old Muslim landlords, who held their position under government title, were still in possession of large sections of Bengal, Bihar, Orissa, and the United Provinces, but in other respects Hindus had the better status. It was inevitable that this situation should produce inter-community middle-class jealousy.

A Single Indian Nation

JAWAHARLAL NEHRU

Statesman, orator, and author, Jawaharlal Nehru dominated, symbolized, and led newly independent India from 1947 to his death in 1964. Before that he had fought passionately for Indian freedom. He was committed to a unified India, governed as a secular democracy, and he vigorously opposed the argument that India was made up of two nations, one Hindu, the other Muslim. For Nehru, there was but one nation, and the communal problem was mainly artificial and contrived, the deliberate policy of the British who sought to divide and rule India. As a socialist, he saw in the Hindu-Muslim quarrel, insofar as it was genuine, the sinister influence of vested feudal interests. The following selections are taken from *The Discovery of India*, a brilliant historical synthesis and interpretation, and his autobiography, *Toward Freedom*. Both books were mainly written in prison.

I T IS . . . wrong and misleading to talk of a Moslem invasion of India or of a Moslem period in India, just as it would be wrong to refer to the coming of the British to India as a Christian invasion, or to call the British period in India a Christian period. Islam did not invade India; it had come to India some centuries earlier. There was a Turkish invasion (Mahmud's), and an Afghan invasion, and then a Turco-Mongol or Moghul invasion; and of these the two latter were important. The Afghans might well be considered a border Indian group, hardly strangers to India, and the period of their political dominance should be called the Indo-Afghan period. The Moghuls were outsiders and strangers to India, and yet they fitted into the Indian structure with remarkable speed and began the Indo-Moghul period.

Through choice or circumstances or both, the Afghan rulers and those who had come with them merged into India. Their dynasties became completely indianized with their roots in India, looking upon India as their homeland and the rest of the world as foreign. . . .

The effect of the Afghan conquest on India and Hinduism was two-fold, each development contradicting the other. The immediate reaction was an exodus of people to the south, away from the areas under Afghan rule. Those who remained became more rigid and exclusive, retired into their shells, and tried to protect themselves from foreign ways and influences by hardening the caste system. On the other hand, there was a gradual and hardly conscious approach toward these foreign ways both in thought and life. A synthesis worked itself

From Jawaharlal Nehru, *The Discovery of India* (New York, 1946), pp. 237–238, and *Toward Freedom* (New York, 1941, published in Britain under the title *Autobiography*), pp. 291–293. Selections from *The Discovery of India* reprinted by permission of The John Day Company, Inc., Asia Publishing House, and Mrs. Indira Nehru-Gandhi; selections from *Toward Freedom* reprinted by permission of The John Day Company, Inc., and The Bodley Head.

19

out: new styles of architecture arose; food and clothing changed, and life was affected and varied in many other ways.

*   *   *

Latterly there has been an interesting development in the speeches and statements of some of the Moslem communal leaders. This has no real importance, and I doubt if many people think so; nevertheless it is significant of the mentality of communalism, and a great deal of prominence has been given to it. Stress has been laid on the "Moslem nation" in India, on "Moslem culture," on the utter incompatibility of Hindu and Moslem "cultures." The inevitable deduction from this is (although it is not put baldly) that the British must remain in India for ever and ever to hold the scales and mediate between the two "cultures."

A few Hindu communal leaders think exactly on the same lines, with this difference, however, that they hope that, being in a majority, their brand of "culture" will ultimately prevail.

Hindu and Moslem "cultures" and the "Moslem nation" — how these words open out fascinating vistas of past history and present and future speculation! The Moslem nation in India — a nation within a nation, and not even compact, but vague, spread out, indeterminate. Politically the idea is absurd; economically it is fantastic; it is hardly worth considering. To talk of a "Moslem nation," therefore, means that there is no nation at all but a religious bond; it means that no nation in the modern sense must be allowed to grow; it means that modern civilization should be discarded and we should go back to the medieval ways; it means either autocratic government or a foreign government; it means, finally, just nothing at all except an emotional state of mind and a conscious or unconscious desire not to face realities, especially economic realities. Emotions have a way of upsetting logic, and we may not ignore them simply because they seem so unreasonable. But this idea of a Moslem nation is the figment of a few imaginations only, and, but for the publicity given to it by the press, few people would have heard of it. And, even if many people believe in it, it would still vanish at the touch of reality.

But what is this "Moslem culture"? Is it a kind of racial memory of the great deeds of the Arabs, Persians, Turks, etc.? Or language? Or art and music? Or customs? I do not remember anyone referring to present-day Moslem art or Moslem music. The two languages which have influenced Moslem thought in India are Arabic and Persian, especially the latter. But the influence of Persia has no element of religion about it. The Persian language and many Persian customs and traditions came to India in the course of thousands of years and impressed themselves powerfully all over north India. Persia was the France of the East, sending its language and culture to all its neighbors. That is a common and precious heritage for all of us in India.

I have tried hard to understand what this "Moslem culture" is, but I confess that I have not succeeded. I find a tiny handful of middle-class Moslems as well as Hindus in north India influenced by the Persian language and traditions. The Moslem peasantry and industrial workers are hardly distinguishable from the Hindu.

II. THE WIDENING COMMUNAL GAP

The Muslim Revival

SIR THEODORE MORISON

Following the British conquest of India and the Mutiny of 1857, the Muslims retreated into an atmosphere of frustration and isolation. The once dynamic rulers of the subcontinent excluded themselves from and ignored the modern forces that were being introduced into India by the British. Sir Theodore Morison describes how this torpor and seeming decadence was transformed largely by the work of a Muslim reformer — Sir Syed Ahmad Khan. Morison describes the Muslim revival and its increasing political consciousness. The author was a distinguished English student and admirer of Muslim civilization and was from 1899 to 1905 the Principal of Aligarh College.

. . . In 1857 came the catastrophe of the Mutiny, for which the English believed, wrongly, that the Muslims were mainly responsible; the phantom sovereignty of the Mogul Emperor was abolished, the noble families which had followed his fallen fortunes were ruined or dispersed, and Delhi ceased to be a Muslim city. All over India Muslim civilization was in evident decay. The Maulvis, the religious leaders of the people, from a mistaken loyalty to Islam, forbade their followers under pain of eternal damnation from acquiring the learning of the *Firanghi* (Franks, i.e., Europeans). The Muslims were thereby excluded from all the liberal professions. For the public services a knowledge of English had now become indispensable; law, medicine, and engineering had been revolutionized by the introduction of European ideas and could only be studied to any purpose in English text-books. While Bengali Hindus, Madra-sis, and Marathas inspired by the arts and sciences of Europe were experiencing an intellectual and moral renaissance, the Muslims all over India were falling into a state of material indigence and intellectual decay.

It was in these circumstances that Sir Syed Ahmad Khan (1817–98) started the great movement of thought which was to inspire the Muslims with new life. Sir Syed was first and last a religious reformer; he summoned his people to return to the sanity and simplicity of primitive Islam. He denounced the superstitions and bigotry with which their faith had become encrusted; he told his people that the only instrument which could accomplish this regeneration was education and that education must be on western lines; there was nothing contrary to the principles of Islam, he said, in the acquisition of western learning — as the Maulvis ignorantly pro-

From Sir Theodore Morison, "Muhammadan Movements," in *Political India*, ed. Sir John Cumming (London, 1932), pp. 87–92, 102–105. Reprinted by permission of Oxford University Press.

claimed. Had not the Prophet said: "Go even to the Walls of China for the sake of learning." The English were possessed of arts and sciences more valuable than those of China, and from them the Muslims could learn without danger to their religion, for God himself had said that the true believers would find their best friends in the People of the Book (Christians and Jews). Sir Syed was violently attacked for his courageous opinions and suffered much social persecution, but no persecution could daunt his leonine courage; his great personality prevailed at length over opposition and misrepresentation, and in the last years of his life he exercised a marvellous ascendancy over Muslim opinion. When he was laid to rest by the side of the mosque of the college in Aligarh, a lifelong friend of his said to me:

Other men have written books and founded colleges; but to arrest as with a wall the degeneration of a whole people, that is the work of a prophet.

That remark conveys, in my opinion, a correct judgement of Sir Syed's personality and of the quality of his work. For myself I can say that I have never met another man so great as he.

Sir Syed was frequently summoned to the Legislative Council of the Governor-General and he had considerable influence upon public policy, but he abstained from political propaganda, which he condemned as dangerous to the country and undesirable for his own people, because it was likely to deflect them from the task of moral and intellectual regeneration — the only thing that mattered. When, however, the Indian National Congress began to criticize the Government and demand the establishment of representative institutions in India upon the pattern of western democracy, he felt obliged to speak out. At Lucknow on 28 December 1887, when the National Congress was holding its third session in Madras, he warned the Muslims of the evils which they would suffer from majority rule and of the bloody consequences of political agitation. He told his hearers that in the existing state of communal temper, Muslims would always vote for a Muslim candidate at the polls and Hindus for a Hindu candidate; and as the Hindus formed the majority of the population no Muslim would ever be elected. But though he recognized the unhappy state of feeling between Hindus and Muslims he deplored it. "There is no person," he said, shortly after his Lucknow speech, "who desires more than I that friendship and union should exist between the two peoples of India and that one should help the other. I have often said that India is like a bride whose two eyes are the Hindus and Muslims. Her beauty consists in this that her two eyes be of equal lustre." And he went on to say:

I have often given my nation to understand that slaughtering cows for the purpose of annoying Hindus is the height of cantankerous folly; if friendship may exist between us and them, that friendship is far to be preferred to the sacrifice of cows.

Sir Syed Ahmad died in 1898, but the political opinions of which he disapproved suffered no abatement. The demand for representative institutions grew more insistent, and it became apparent that English opinion was favourable to this method of enlarging Indian liberties. The Muslims became so seriously concerned that in 1906 they took a deputation to the Viceroy, Lord Minto, and requested that, if this form of government should be introduced into India, Muslims should be protected by special safeguards; they laid particular stress upon their demand for separate electorates, that is, for the right of themselves electing their own representatives upon municipalities, rural boards, and provincial legislatures. Lord Minto expressed his agreement with the principle for which they contended, and was thus the first to give the Muslims a pledge to which they attach great importance and which has since been often repeated. By their visit to Simla, the leaders of the Muslim community were so convinced that serious changes were impending that they resolved to abandon their aloofness from popular politics, and in December 1906 they founded the All-India Muslim League. From this time forward the Muslims have been an organized party in Indian politics.

Events soon showed the need for some such organization. Very shortly afterwards, the extension of Indian liberties, commonly known as the Morley-Minto reforms, became the subject of public discussion, and the All-India Muslim League was the agency by which vigorous representations were made both in India and in England. The points upon which special emphasis was laid were that in any system of representation introduced into India (1) the Muslims should have the right of electing their own representatives by means of special electorates, and (2) the number of seats allotted to Muslims should be in excess of their ratio to the general population. The grounds upon which they based the first claim were:

(a) In the existing state of tension between the two great communities, no Muslim who sincerely represented the opinions of his community could secure election in a general (i.e., mixed or joint) electorate, since in all but two provinces the Muslims were a minority of the population.

(b) If the two communities were not kept apart at the polls every contested election would result in communal riots, accompanied by bloodshed, and would leave bitter memories, which would retard the political integration of the country.

(c) Where the system of separate electorates had been established in municipalities and district boards, it had worked well and secured peace; it had been devised empirically by British officers in order to avoid recurrent disturbances at election times and had in fact proved successful.

The grounds upon which the Muslims based their second claim was that they did in fact command an amount of influence which was greatly in excess of their ratio to the population. In spite of retrogression in recent years, they still owned much of the landed property in India, they still formed a very large element in the public service, and Muslim soldiers constituted a large proportion of the Indian Army. By the geographical distribution of the Muslim population they were the gatekeepers of India, and upon them must fall the principal burden of repelling a foreign invasion. They confessed that owing to a mistaken interpretation of the behests of their religion they had lagged behind others in English education, but maintained that their ascendancy, due to historical causes, was a fact which could not be ignored in estimating public opinion.

These claims were combated by the Hindu politicians of the Congress, but were accepted as valid by the Government of India, by the Secretary of State, and by the House of Commons. . . .

A review of the political activities of the Indian Muslims during the last half-century shows them to have pursued a fairly consistent policy. They have resented the treatment of Indians as an inferior race and have claimed association in the government on terms of absolute equality. They have supported all measures for liberalizing the administration though not by methods of agitation and terrorism. On the other hand, they have never shown much enthusiasm for popular government. Within their own community, social democracy exists to an extent not yet achieved in England, but of political democracy they are sceptical. From the days of their ascendancy they have inherited a very sane and objective conception of the duties and difficulties of governing a country. They know that the great masses of the Indian population are uneducated and particularly liable to gusts of passion and religious emotion — their own community not excepted: they are not, therefore, easily convinced of the wisdom of entrusting the fortunes of the State to such hands. However, as the British refused, on the one hand, to admit Indians to the higher ranks of the Civil Service and the Army, and, on the other, were positively eager to extend popular (i.e., Indian) control on municipal boards, district boards, and legislatures, they accepted this as the only line of advance open to them. But as soon as it became clear that policy was to be determined by popular vote, they were compelled to consider very seriously what sort of a position they as a community would hold in the India of the future. For this reason their political activities have in the main been devoted to the elaboration of safeguards which would secure them from oppression by a hostile majority, but they have found it very difficult to convince public opinion in England and in India of the necessity or desirability of these precautions. . . .

It is useless to enumerate the grounds of difference between Hindu and Muslim; the only thing that matters is that they do in fact feel and think of themselves as separate peoples. In all disquisitions on nationality this is the only test which is found to cover all cases. If a certain body of persons think of themselves as one nation and are willing to endure tribulation and material losses in order to remain together, then they are one people; if they cannot pass this acid test, they are not. Judged by this standard the Muslims of India are a nation. Communal differences, as they are called, are really national jealousies. That is why Sir Muhammad Iqbal declared "the problem of India is international, not national."

The Long Record of Communal Antagonism

SIR HUGH MACPHERSON

Those who argued, as did Nehru, that communal tension was a product of British rule insisted that the outbreaks of violence between the two groups that became common in the twentieth century were a new phenomenon. It is this charge that Sir Hugh MacPherson, a member of the Indian Civil Service, was attempting to answer in the following passage. He lists a number of instances of strife in the nineteenth century, some at a time when British rule had not been established.

MacPherson served in India for many years, holding many important posts including that of provincial governor. He made a firsthand study of Hindu-Muslim relations among the peasantry.

THE differences which separate Hindu and Muslim are essentially religious. They may be reinforced by historical tradition, by political rivalries, or by economic contrasts, but for the great masses of the population it is the religious issue alone that counts. The Hindu has many gods in his universe; he reverences the Brahmin; he venerates the cow; and he makes joyful music at his festivals. The Muslim is monotheistic; he is a follower of the Prophet; he reverences the Koran; he excludes music from the mosque. Once a year at the Bakr-Id festival he sacrifices a cow. The slaughter of kine excites the Hindu, and has been the proximate cause of communal rioting in nine cases out of ten. Disturbance of mosque prayers by passing bands of Hindu processionists rouses the darkest passions of Muslim worshippers and has been a frequent preliminary to serious disorder, especially in the larger cities during the last twenty years. Disputes regarding the sites of sacred buildings have been another source of trouble, and a still more fertile cause has been the clash of rival processions. By reason of their different calendars the dates of important Hindu and Muslim festivals coincide in cycles of years, and the possibilities of hostile collision are then greatly increased.

Such purely religious causes explain most of the communal disturbances of which we have record in the earlier years of British rule. Before that time Benares had been a storm centre, since Aurangzeb built his famous mosque there on the site of an old Hindu temple. In October 1809 there was here a sudden outbreak of great intensity, when Hindu mobs stormed the mosque and put to death every Muslim of the neighbourhood who fell into their hands.

The entire city was given up to pillage and slaughter: and order was not restored by the troops until some fifty mosques had been destroyed and several hundred people had lost their lives.

From Sir Hugh MacPherson, "The Origin and Growth of Communal Antagonism," in *Political India*, ed. Sir John Cumming (London, 1932), pp. 109–116. Reprinted by permission of Oxford University Press.

In 1871–2 two important Muslim and Hindu festivals clashed and there were riots with heavy casualties at Bareilly and other centres in the United Provinces, culminating in the great Delhi riots of 1886. In June 1893 grave outbreaks occurred in the Azamgarh district of the United Provinces in connexion with cow-killing at the Bakr-Id, and in August of the same year there were very serious Muharram riots at Bombay which lasted for six days; eighty persons lost their lives, many mosques and temples were desecrated, and many shops were pillaged.

These older instances of communal trouble are mentioned because it is sometimes suggested that communal collisions are a modern invention, the product of recent political developments. At the second session of the Round Table Conference Mr. Gandhi declared that the quarrel between Hindu and Muhammadan is "coeval with the British advent" and that it will dissolve when the peoples of India are free. A sufficient answer has been supplied by one of the great landholders of Bengal, who writes:

The fact is that the religious and cultural feuds between Hindus and Mohammedans go as far back as A.D. 1017 or 1018, when Mahmud of Ghazni conquered the then Hindu centre of India, known as Kanauj, desecrated the holy city of Muttra and destroyed and pillaged many Hindu temples. Mahmud thus sowed the seeds of hatred and religious animosity which have survived through the ages, bringing a bitterness between Hindus and Mohammedans which breaks out at any moment. . . .

It was after the Bombay riots of 1893 that Mr. Bal Gangadhar Tilak started his "Anti-Cow-Killing Society" and began to organize other propaganda, anti-British and anti-Muhammadan, which were designed to stimulate the militant spirit of Hinduism and establish its domination of the Indian political world. The religious basis of communal dissension began from this date to be reinforced by political factors. As explained [elsewhere] Muhammad-ans, following the advice of their great leader, Sir Syed Ahmad Khan, with few exceptions held aloof from the political agitation centred from 1885 onwards in the Indian National Congress. This dissociation was in itself a cause of estrangement between the two communities. Under the influence of the same leader they abandoned their opposition to western education and began to take part more earnestly in the competition for public appointments. In the earliest days of British rule they had been in possession of this field as a heritage from the Mogul empire, but after 1837, when Persian was superseded by the vernaculars in the subordinate courts and by English in the higher offices, they were gradually displaced by Hindus. The Mutiny in 1857 added to their discomfiture, as the blame largely fell on them; but in 1873 the question of Muhammadan education was reviewed by Government, their disabilities and grievances were recognized, and measures were taken to remove them. Since that date Muslims have made steady progress, but they still have much leeway to make up in their more backward centres of Bengal, the Punjab, and Sind. The competition for government service thus stimulated is one of the healthier communal rivalries which finds frequent expression in the provincial legislatures.

In 1906 . . . the Muslim League was founded to protect Muhammadan interests, and in response to demands soon after formulated, the principle of separate representation in the provincial and central legislatures, weighted to allow for their political importance, was conceded to Muhammadans in the Morley-Minto reforms of 1909. This principle has been ever since a source of dispute and negotiation between Hindu and Muslim politicians, but remains firmly established in spite of all attempted compromises.

The partition of Bengal in 1905, though it aroused intense feeling amongst the Hindus of the province, was welcomed by the backward Muhammadans of the eastern districts, to whom it gave new hope. They took no part in the violent agitation, the boycott of British goods, and the revolutionary outrages which followed. On the contrary they resented the tactics of the Hindus, and the conflict came to a head in the dangerous Mymensingh disturbances of May 1907, which took the form of a general rising of the Muhammadan peasantry against their Hindu landlords and creditors. The reversal of the partition in 1911 was a profound disappointment to the Muslim community throughout India. The revulsion of feeling thus caused, combined with their reaction to Turkey's misfortunes in Tripoli, chilled their attitude towards Government and encouraged that *rapprochement* between the Muslim League and the National Congress which was to bear fruit later in the Lucknow Pact of 1916. The entry of Turkey into the War on the side of the enemy powers placed a further burden on the sympathies of Indian Muslims, and it is everlastingly to their credit that their loyalty stood the strain, except for a small pan-Islamic group which had to be kept under restraint during the War and was to give much trouble after it was over.

The great masses of the population, both Hindu and Muhammadan, cared little for the manoeuvres of the politicians or the reactions of the War, and a sinister event was soon to happen which showed that for them the old religious antagonism was still a compelling force in their lives. In 1915 and again in 1916 there had been serious riots in the Patna district of Bihar over cow-sacrifice at the Bakr-Id festival. During the rains of 1917, when the rice fields were full of water, trouble broke out unexpectedly in the adjoining district of Shahabad. For more than a fortnight large Hindu mobs wandered over a tract of some 2,000 square miles, attacking, burning, and pillaging Muslim villages and houses, retreating before the police through the flooded fields, and re-forming for fresh outrages. Nearly 2,000 police and troops, infantry and cavalry, had to be poured into the district before the rising was subdued.

The brutalities practised on the unfortunate victims of these riots were the theme of indignation meetings in many mosques of northern India, and collections were made in aid of the sufferers wherever there were Muhammadans.

The punishment of the Hindu aggressors which followed was swift and stern. The bitter memories of 1917 left no room later for an anti-Government alliance between the Hindu and Muhammadan masses of Bihar.

Except for a savage outbreak at Katarput (United Provinces) in 1918, there was a lull in communal strife for the next four years. The Montagu-Chelmsford Report, the measures adopted to deal with the revolutionary movement and the Punjab disturbances occupied the public mind. Muhammadans were full of apprehension regarding the fate of Turkey, and Mr. Gandhi seized this opportunity to forge an alliance with the pan-Islamic leaders of the Khilafat Committee and to enlist their fiery aid in his first non-co-operation campaign. With the progress of that campaign we are not here concerned. The alliance received a mortal blow when the Moplah rebellion broke out in the Malabar district of Madras in the autumn of 1921, and these savage fanatical Muslims of mixed Arab descent turned all their fury on their Hindu neighbours.

Murders, forcible conversions, desecrations of temples, outrages upon women, pillage, arson and destruction were perpetrated freely, until troops could be assembled for the task of restoring order in a difficult and extensive tract of country. As might be expected, the barbarities practised by the Moplahs had immediate reactions on Hindu and Muslim relations throughout India.

By the middle of 1922 the alliance between the Hindu and Muhammadan extremists had completely broken down, the non-co-operation campaign had failed and the Khilafat grievance vanished when

Turkey deposed the Khalifa and settled her affairs in her own way. The old religious dissensions between the two communities were now being stimulated by proselytizing activities. On the part of the Hindus there were two movements: one which sought to bring back to the Hindu fold converts to Islam and Christianity; and another, whose object was to foster militant Hinduism. The Muhammadans replied with counter-organizations, and the operations of these opposing movements did much to heat the communal atmosphere.

The first grave outbreak of a new series occurred at Multan (Punjab) in September 1922 on the occasion of the Muharram festival, and the celebrations in 1923 were marked by serious collisions, of which the most formidable occurred at Saharanpur (United Provinces), where the casualties exceeded 300. The year 1924 had a still blacker record with 18 serious riots, in which 86 persons were killed and 776 wounded. The worst storm centre was Kohat in the Frontier Province, where terrible disturbances arose out of the publication of an anti-Islamic poem of Hindu authorship. The roll of two days' casualties amounted to 36 killed and 145 wounded: extensive looting took place in the bazaars, and house property valued at £70,000 was destroyed. The riots were followed by a temporary exodus from the town of the entire Hindu population. The Kohat tragedy sent a thrill of horror throughout India, and a conference attended by leading representatives of all creeds was held at Delhi in September 1924 to concert peace measures. There was some improvement in 1925, but it was short-lived, for all previous records were surpassed in 1926 with 36 serious riots and a casualty roll of close on 2,000. In this year Calcutta took the lead with disturbances which started over the old trouble of music before mosques and developed into an orgy of murderous attacks by hooligans of both camps. Before peace was finally restored 200 shops were looted, 12 sacred buildings were desecrated

or destroyed, there were 150 cases of incendiary fire and 1,450 casualties, including 140 deaths.

In previous years religious disputes had been the chief causes of collision, but the tension had now become so great that the most trivial incidents sufficed to start trouble. The demon of unrest was abroad; the spirit of lawlessness had been aroused by the non-co-operation movement; and communal disorder had become the dominant factor of Indian political life. . . . After a short lull of a few months the mischief revived with unabated vigour, and the year 1927 was almost as black as its predecessor. Thirty-one serious riots occurred with a casualty roll exceeding 1,600. . . .

Communal riots were much less frequent in 1928 than in the two previous years, but between February and May 1929 there occurred serious disturbances in Bombay City, which began with collisions between Hindu strikers and Pathan substitutes, and continued as in Calcutta three years before, with murderous assaults on individuals and wholesale looting of shops by the criminal classes. Before the disorder finally subsided there had been over 1,100 casualties, including nearly 200 deaths. The significance of these riots was that their proximate cause was economic rather than religious.

The Viceroy's announcement of 31 October 1929 regarding Dominion status and the Round Table Conference rallied moderate opinion throughout India, but did not prevent the extremists from launching their second campaign of civil disobedience in the spring of the following year. This disastrous war against authority widened the breach between Hindus and Muhammadans, for the latter resented the tyrannous interference with their normal activities exercised by the Congress agents. A temporary halt was called on 4 March 1931, but the ink was hardly dry on the Delhi agreement when the Cawnpore tragedy shocked the whole of India. In the course of an enforced closing of shops, in honour of a Hindu assassin, the Hindus and Muhammadans of Cawnpore came to blows.

This developed into a riot of unprecedented violence and peculiar atrocity. . . . Murders, arson and looting were widespread for three days. . . . The death roll . . . was probably between four and five hundred — a large number of temples and mosques were desecrated or destroyed, and a very large number of houses were burnt and pillaged.

In the spring of 1932 political tension between the Hindu and Muslim communities greatly increased throughout India. The Round Table Conference had failed to settle the communal issue, Congress had resumed its activities and all parties awaited with nervousness the communal award expected of Government. About the middle of May a petty quarrel between Muslim and Hindu youths started a conflagration in the much-troubled city of Bombay. The guerilla warfare which followed took the usual form of murderous assaults, pillage of shops, and incendiary fires. Before order was finally restored by the troops and the police, nearly 3,000 casualties, including over 200 deaths, had occurred. Competent observers held that the bitterness was greater than in 1929 and was marked by political rather than religious manifestations.

This brief record of communal conflicts, in which only the most prominent incidents have been mentioned, forms a dark page in Indian history. If it has been blacker during the past decade, the cause is doubtless to be found, partly in the unrest produced in the minds of the masses by the ceaseless agitation of these later years, and partly in the general uneasiness induced in all minds by the fear of impending changes in the constitutional structure. Two comments of a general nature may be made. The record would have been many times blacker if the areas of

disturbance and the extent of the casualties had not been closely limited by the united efforts of the magistracy, the police, and the military. Throughout these troubles the conduct of the police and of the troops has won the highest praise. Few, if any, of the major conflicts have been brought under control without the aid of the military, and it is impossible to exaggerate the relief and confidence which the arrival and presence of troops has inspired in the attacked minority.

On the other hand, one must guard against the cumulative effect of a bare recital of the facts. To get the picture in proper perspective, one must stand back from the canvas and remember that the facts are culled from a sub-continent, from a population of 250 millions in British India living in half a million villages and some 1,600 towns and cities. The toll of human life from communal conflicts during the past sixty years has been less than the holocaust of a single massacre in the olden days.

The great masses of the rural population, whether Hindu or Muhammadan, are simple cultivators, who at all normal times live in peace and amity. Their chief pre-occupations are the timely arrival and seasonal distribution of the annual rains, the tillage of their fields, the gathering of their harvests, their dealings with their landlords and their money-lenders. Religious festivals are one of their few excitements. If these occasionally lead to strife and bloodshed, normal relations are resumed as soon as the lava flow of passion subsides. The urban masses are more prone to communal strife, because life is more complicated in the towns. Here political friction often stimulates religious antagonism; temples and mosques are closer together; there is more danger of collision in the narrow streets, and a larger admixture of the rowdy turbulent elements that love disorder for its own sake and for its opportunities. The educated classes of both communities, when their vision is not temporarily clouded by some communal issue, work harmoniously together in all walks of life. It may indeed be claimed with justice that they have been drawn together, not severed, by their century and a half of association under a common administration, which has given them the same laws, the same security of person and freedom of action, the same schools and universities, the same progressive civilization and the bond of a common speech.

An Official British View on Communal Electorates

MONTAGU-CHELMSFORD REPORT

Much has been written on the pros and cons of communal electorates. The following British statement presents the official view of Edward Montagu, Secretary of State for India, and Lord Chelmsford, the Governor-General, as contained in the famous *Report on Indian Constitutional Reforms* (1918). It will be seen that these officials decry this type of electorate, declaring such communal separation as divisive. Such a practice, in their view, will act as a serious hindrance to the development of a self-governing India. On the grounds of practical necessity, however, they recommend retention of this device, pointing out that the abolition of communal electorates would be considered a breach of faith by Muslims and also a danger to their interests.

AT THIS POINT we are brought face to face with the most difficult question which arises in connexion with elected assemblies — whether communal electorates are to be maintained. We may be told that this is a closed question, because the Muhammadans will never agree to any revision of the arrangement promised them by Lord Minto in 1906, and secured to them by the reforms of 1909. But we have felt bound to re-examine the question fully in the light of our new policy; and also because we have been pressed to extend the system of communal electorates in a variety of directions. This is no new problem. It has been discussed periodically from the time when the first steps were taken to liberalise the councils. . . .

The crucial test to which, as we conceive, all proposals should be brought is whether they will or will not help to carry India towards responsible government. Some persons hold that for a people such as they deem those of India to be, so divided by race, religion and caste as to be unable to consider the interests of any but their own section, a system of communal and class representation is not merely inevitable but is actually best. . . . But when we consider what responsible government implies, and how it was developed in the world we cannot take this view. . . .

We conclude unhesitatingly that the history of self-government among the nations who developed it and spread it through the world is decisively against the admission by the State of any divided allegiance; against the State's arranging its members in any way which encourages them to think of themselves primarily as citizens of any smaller unit than itself. . . .

Division by creeds and classes means the creation of political camps organised against each other, and teaches men to think as partisans and not as citizens; and it is difficult to see how the change from this system to national representation is ever to occur. The British Government is often accused of dividing men in order to govern them. But if it unnecessarily divides them at the very moment when it professes to start them on the road to gov-

From Cd. 9109, *Report on Indian Constitutional Reforms* (London: His Majesty's Stationery Office, 1918), pp. 185–188.

31

erning themselves, it will find it difficult to meet the charge of being hypocritical or short sighted. . . .

We regard any system of communal electorates, therefore, as a very serious hindrance to the development of the self-governing principle. The evils of any extension of the system are plain. . . . At the same time we must face the hard facts. The Muhammadans were given special representation with separate electorates in 1909. The Hindus' acquiescence is embodied in the present agreement between the political leaders of the two communities (the so-called Lucknow Pact of 1916). The Muhammadans regard these as settled facts, and any attempt to go back on them would rouse a storm of bitter protest and put a severe strain on the loyalty of a community which has behaved with conspicuous loyalty during a period of great difficulty, and which we know to be feeling no small anxiety for its own welfare under a system of popular government. The Muham-madans regard separate representation and communal electorates as their only adequate safeguards. But apart from a pledge which we must honour until we are released from it, we are bound to see that the community secures proper representation in the new councils. How can we say to them that we regard the decision of 1909 as mistaken, that its retention is incompatible with progress towards responsible government, that its reversal will eventually be to their benefit; and that for these reasons we have decided to go back on it? Much as we regret the necessity, we are convinced that so far as the Muhammadans at all events are concerned the present system must be maintained until conditions alter, even at the price of slower progress towards the realisation of a common citizenship. But we can see no reason to set up communal representation for Muhammadans in any province where they form a majority of the voters.

Hindu-Muslim Rivalry: A Struggle for Political Power

THE INDIAN STATUTORY (SIMON) COMMISSION

As the 1920's ended, the British Government appointed a Commission to review the situation in India and to make an investigation into the working of the system of government with a view to its reform and liberalization. After an exhaustive study on the spot the Royal Commission published a two-volume *Report*, the first part of which was an invaluable survey of political, social, and educational conditions. The following passages describe in general terms the dichotomy between the Hindu and Muslim communities. The mounting instances of communal feuds after World War I are listed together with appeals made by the Governor-General, Lord Irwin, for an end to these outbreaks. The issue of separate electorates is examined and dismissed as an important cause of the problem. Rather the Commission asserts that back of the rivalry is the struggle for political power. As long as British rule gave no sign of abdication there was no trouble; but as soon as it became evident that this power would be increasingly shared, Hindu-Muslim rivalry mounted.

DISPERSED among the 216 millions of Hindus of India are nearly 70 million representatives of a widely different type of culture, not originally or exclusively Indian, but spread throughout India as a consequence of a series of invasions from the North and West which have taken place within historic times. The splendid monuments of Mogul architecture stand as a perpetual reminder of the vanished domination of Muhammadan rule. Yet during the centuries when the material power of Islam was at its highest in India, it was quite unable to crush the enduring influences of Hinduism. When British authority began to extend over the Indian continent it could, as a neutral, set up and endeavour to apply a canon of tolerance, but it could not alter the essential facts of Hindu-Moslem difference. It would be an utter misapprehension to suppose that Hindu-Moslem antagonism is analogous to the separation between religious denominations in contemporary Europe. Differences of race, a different system of law, and the absence of intermarriage constitute a far more effective barrier. It is a basic opposition manifesting itself at every turn in social custom and economic competition, as well as in mutual religious antipathy. Today, in spite of much neighbourly kindliness in ordinary affairs, and notwithstanding all the efforts made by men of good will in both communities to promote Hindu-Moslem concord, the rivalry and dissension between these two forces are one of the chief stumbling blocks in the way of smoother and more rapid progress. We regard it as an essential part of our task (as in due course it will be a vital concern of Parliament) to make an impartial survey of the guiding facts of this situation before approaching the question of the method of its constitutional treatment.

If we confine ourselves for the moment

From Cd. 3568, *Report of the Indian Statutory Commission.* Vol. I (London: His Majesty's Stationery Office, 1930), pp. 24–30.

33

to British India, the Hindu population amounts to 163 millions and the Muhammadans to approximately 59½ millions. In two of the Governors' Provinces, Muhammadans are in an actual majority; their total in Bengal amounts to 25,210,000 out of the 47 millions which that province contains, and in the Punjab Muhammadans are enumerated at 11,400,000 out of a total of just over 20 millions. In the other seven provinces to which the Reforms have been applied they are everywhere in a minority. In Assam they are 28 per cent of the population; in Bombay 19 per cent; in the United Provinces 14 per cent; in Bihar and Orissa 10 per cent; and in Madras just over 6 per cent. In the Central Provinces they amount to only half a million out of a total population of nearly 14 millions; and out of Burma's 13 millions (of which more than 11 millions are Buddhists) they muster half a million. One of the difficulties, therefore, in adjusting representation in the provincial legislatures — unless for this purpose religious divisions are to be disregarded — is to devise a scheme which takes due account of Muhammadan predominance where it is found to occur, and at the same time provides adequate representation where Moslems are in a minority. It is an elementary reflection, but one not always borne in mind, that weightage in favour of one interest necessarily involves a reduction in the proportionate representation of the rest. In the North West Frontier Province Muhammadans are in a large majority (over 2 millions out of a total of 2¼ millions in the administered territory); and in the administered area of Baluchistan they amount to 367,000 out of a total of 420,000.

Turning to the Indian States, the total Hindu population is 53½ millions, and the total Muhammadan population 9¼ millions. Muhammadans are in a majority in Kashmir, though the ruling house is Hindu. On the other hand, Hyderabad, with a total population of 12½ millions, of which more than 10½ millions are Hindus, has as its ruler the Nizam, who is a Muhammadan.

CAUSES OF HINDU-MOSLEM TENSION

It is evident, therefore, that the distribution of the population as between Hindus and Muhammadans provides one of the most serious complications for Indian statesmanship, and that this question recurs in different forms and degrees in almost every part of India. The minority community is not concentrated in one part of the area, as Protestants in Ireland tend to be concentrated in Ulster. It is mainly represented in the North-Western parts of India and in Eastern Bengal, but its numbers elsewhere are not sufficiently small to be disregarded, and not sufficiently large to claim the mastery of numbers. These being the statistical facts, we must now proceed to give the best account we can of the nature of the antagonisms which these rival communities tend to develop, of the extent to which this tension is growing or dying away, and of the influence which these considerations are bound to exercise upon the treatment of the constitutional problem. It unfortunately happens that on Indian soil the opposition of these two faiths is sharply intensified by religious practices which are only too likely to provoke mutual ill-feeling. The devout Hindu regards the cow as an object of great veneration, while the ceremonial sacrifice of cows or other animals is a feature of the annual Muhammadan festival known as the Baqr'Id. Hindu music played through the streets on the occasion of the procession of an idol, or in connection with a marriage celebration, may take place at a time when the Muhammadans of the town are at worship in an adjoining mosque, and hence arises an outbreak of resentment which is apt to degenerate into a serious quarrel. The religious anniversaries observed by Moslems are fixed by reference to a lunar year which does not correspond with the adjusted Hindu calendar, and consequently it occasionally happens that dates of special importance in the two religions coincide — as, for instance, when an anniversary of Moslem mourning synchronises with a day of Hindu rejoicing —

and the authorities responsible for the maintenance of law and order are then faced with a time of special anxiety. In spite of the constant watchfulness of the police authorities, and of the earnest efforts of leaders in both communities to reach a *modus vivendi*, the immediate occasion of communal disorder is nearly always the religious issue. On the other hand, when communal feeling is roused on some matter of secular interest, religious zeal is always present to stimulate conflict, and partisans are not slow to exploit the opportunity.

THE PRESENT STATE
OF COMMUNAL FEELING

It is a lamentable fact that the occasions when Hindu-Muhammadan tension is carried to the point of violent outbreak have not diminished since the Reforms. In the five years 1923 to 1927 approximately 45 lives have been lost and 5,000 persons have been injured in communal riots; these figures include some disturbances in which Sikhs were involved. A statement laid on the table of the Legislative Assembly showed that from September 1927 to June 1928 there had been 19 serious Hindu-Muhammadan riots, which had affected every province except Madras. It would serve no useful purpose to reproduce in this Report the details with which we have been supplied; the facts are undeniable, and it is not surprising that Lord Irwin, in his striking appeal soon after he first set foot in India, to the leaders of the two communities to co-operate in a new effort to cope with the evil, should have declared that Hindu-Muhammadan antagonism was "so clearly the dominant issue in Indian life." Every well-wisher of India's constitutional progress must be deeply stirred by the Viceroy's words:

Let the leaders and thoughtful men in each community, the Hindu among the Hindus, and Moslem among the Moslems, throw themselves with ardour into a new form of communal work and into a nobler struggle, and fight for toleration. I do not believe that the task is beyond their powers. I see before me two ancient and highly organised societies with able and esteemed public men as their recognised leaders. I cannot conceive that a really sincere and sustained appeal by them to the rank and file of their co-religionists sustained by active propaganda of the new gospel of peace would pass unheeded. . . . In the name of Indian national life, in the name of religion, I appeal to all in each of the two communities who hold position, who represent them in the press, who direct the education of the young, who possess influence, who command the esteem of their co-religionists, who lead them in politics or are honoured by them as divines. Let them begin each in their own community to work untiringly towards this end; boldly to repudiate feelings of hatred and intolerance, actively to condemn and suppress acts of violence and aggression, earnestly to strive to exorcise suspicions and misapprehensions and so create a new atmosphere of trust. . . .

Lord Irwin repeated his warning and his appeal at the opening of the Simla session of the Indian Legislature on the 29th August, 1927:

I am not exaggerating when I say that, during the 17 months that I have been in India, the whole landscape has been over-shadowed by the lowering clouds of communal tension, which have repeatedly discharged their thunderbolts, spreading far throughout the land their devastating havoc. From April to July last year Calcutta seemed to be under the mastery of some evil spirit, which so gripped the minds of men that in their insanity they held themselves absolved from the most sacred restraints of human conduct. Since then we have seen the same sinister influences at work in Pabna, Rawalpindi, Lahore and many other places, and have been forced to look upon that abyss of unchained human passions that lies too often beneath the surface of habit and of law. In less than 18 months, so far as numbers are available, the toll taken by this bloody strife has been between 250 and 300 killed, and over 2,500 injured. . . . United must be the effort if it is to gain success; and on the successful issue of such work depends the building of the Indian Nation. . . .

We are far from saying that these appeals have met with no response, for the leaders of both communities are deeply conscious of the truth of the Viceroy's words, and of the injury that is being done by the continuance of communal tension. But the Report of the Bombay Riots Inquiry Committee published in August last, observes that since the date of the speech just quoted, at least 20 serious communal riots have occurred in various parts of India, the two Bombay riots alone accounting for the deaths of nearly 200 persons. It is noteworthy that in Bombay, where Hindu-Muhammadan tension does not normally exist to the extent to which it is often found in Calcutta, the origin of the recent riots was not communal, but was to be found in inflammatory speeches made by extremist leaders during a textile strike, followed by an outbreak of wild rumour and isolated murders, after which communal feeling was inevitably aroused.

INFLUENCE OF THE REFORMS ON COMMUNAL RIVALRY

The question has been raised whether Hindu-Muhammadan tension is aggravated or assuaged by the prevailing system of communal representation, under which Moslem voters form a separate electoral roll and choose their own members (as the Sikhs also do in the Punjab), while non-Muhammadan electors are grouped in distinct constituencies and elect their own representatives. On the one hand it is contended that this separation actually reduces the chances of conflict, as the rival communities are not fighting against one another for the same seats, but each is concerned solely with selection from inside its own body. On the other hand it is argued that such an arrangement tends to encourage the appeal to communal sentiment, instead of developing political associations along the lines of a broader citizenship. There is a long and important history connected with the separate representation of Muhammadans which needs to be carefully studied before detailed proposals for the future can be discussed or put forward.

But we may say at once that in our judgment communal representation cannot be justly regarded as the reason for the communal tension we have been describing, and there is no solid ground for supposing that if communal representation were abolished communal strife would disappear. The true cause lies deeper and arises from conditions which are far more difficult to change than the mechanics of representation.

In so far as this tension is due to the constitutional situation, it is not to be explained by dwelling upon the operation of electoral arrangements, but is a manifestation of the anxieties and ambitions aroused in both communities by the prospect of India's political future. So long as authority was firmly established in British hands, and self-government was not thought of, Hindu-Moslem rivalry was confined within a narrower field. This was not merely because the presence of a neutral bureaucracy discouraged strife. A further reason was that there was little for members of one community to fear from the predominance of the other. The comparative absence of communal strife in the Indian States to-day may be similarly explained. Many who are well acquainted with conditions in British India a generation ago would testify that at that epoch so much good feeling had been engendered between the two sides that communal tension as a threat to civil peace was at a minimum. But the coming of the Reforms and the anticipation of what may follow them have given new point to Hindu-Moslem competition. A great part of the evidence given before us was on communal lines, and the same cleavage appears in the Reports of the Indian Committees that sat with us. The one community naturally lays claim to the rights of a majority and relies upon its qualifications of better education and greater wealth; the other is all the more determined on those accounts to secure effective protection for its members, and does not forget that it represents the previous conquerors of the country. It wishes to be assured of adequate representation and of a full share of official posts.

Hence has arisen a situation which it is of the most urgent importance for the influences which operate on public opinion in India to relieve. But no cure is likely to be found by ascribing false causes to the disease. The true cause, as it seems to us, is the struggle for political power and for the opportunities which political power confers. We are fully alive to the arguments against communal representation, but we cannot think that it is the effective cause of this deplorable friction. At the same time we are no less clearly convinced that separate communal electorates serve to perpetuate political divisions on purely communal lines, and we have every sympathy with those who look forward to the day when a growing sense of common citizenship and a general recognition of the rights of minorities will make such arrangements unnecessary. We shall return to this subject, and make our own observations upon it in our second volume. Here we are only concerned to call attention to the facts of a very serious situation, which every well-wisher of India should do his utmost to improve.

Hindu-Muslim Antagonism: A British Creation

JABEZ T. SUNDERLAND

India's struggle for freedom always had many sympathetic supporters in the United States, for whom colonialism in any form was unjustified. The author of the following statement served as President of the India Information Bureau of America, an important agency which before World War II sought support for the Indian nationalist cause. Sunderland was especially active in the 1920's, writing and lecturing in support of Home Rule for India. In this selection from one of his books he seeks to prove that between Hindus and Muslims there is "absolutely nothing fundamentally antagonistic." Whatever rivalry and antipathy exists is created by the British, who use techniques of division, thus preventing a united Indian front and thereby perpetuating their rule.

THERE are in India about seventy millions of Moslems and two hundred ten millions of Hindus.

Disturbing reports come to us from time to time of hostilities and riots between these two great religious communities, sometimes resulting in considerable bloodshed and loss of life. As is well known, these riots are claimed by the British to be clear evidences that their rule in India is necessary, absolutely necessary, to prevent the Mohammedans and Hindus from destroying one another in great numbers, and plunging the country into devastating wars. Is this claim well founded?

As soon as we begin to examine the situation with care and a desire to be unbiased, we discover that there are two exactly opposite views of the case. One is that of the British, just suggested, namely, that the hostilities and riots are very bad; that the responsibility for them rests wholly upon the Indian people; that were it not for the presence of the British Government, the Hindus and Moslems would be at each other's throats and the country would be deluged with blood; and therefore for India's sake, the British must stay.

The other view, which is that of a large part of the most intelligent Indian people, denies that the hostilities and riots are as numerous or serious as the British reports indicate; and, as to responsibility for them, it places that primarily on the British, and only secondarily, if at all, on the Hindus or Moslems.

It puts the case essentially in this way: The Hindus and Moslems of India are not naturally hostile. When left to themselves, that is, when not stirred to hurtful rivalries or to antagonisms by outside influences, they are as kind and peaceful neighbors and friends as are to be found anywhere in the world. Living side by side in nearly all parts of India, no one would know them apart except for possibly some slight difference in dress or in religious practice or rite, which does not affect at all their business relations or their neighborly relations or their friendship and good will to one another. Why then should there be riots between them? Is it not necessary to look for some outside cause?

Wherever in India the British are most

From Jabez T. Sunderland, *India in Bondage* (New York: Lewis Copeland Co.), pp. 229–244.

in evidence there the riots are usually worst; wherever the British are least in evidence, there riots are generally fewest.

Before the British came to India, there seems to have been little hostility between Hindus and Moslems; everywhere they seem to have lived together for the most part peacefully and harmoniously. In the Native States today, where there are few British and where British rule is least felt, there are very few riots, and very little enmity is seen. It is only since British rule in India began, and in those parts of the country where British rule is most directly and strongly felt, that the hostility becomes noticeable and riots of any importance appear.

The only conclusion, therefore, that it seems possible to draw is that, instead of the British being needed in India to prevent hostilities and riots, it is their presence that is mainly responsible for such riots or other hostilities as exist.

Going more into details, the Indian view of the case may be stated somewhat as follows:

The British policy in India has been from the beginning that known as "divide and rule," or that which the old Romans described by their well-known Latin words, *divide et impera*. This has been the policy of all great conquerors and rulers of foreign peoples, from those of ancient Babylonia, Assyria, Persia and Egypt down to Napoleon in Europe and Clive in India. All the British conquerors of India used it, and did not hesitate to boast that they did. Indeed without employing this policy of stirring up hostility between states, between princes, and between parties, and taking the side of one against the other and thus gaining control over both, the British could never have conquered the land. Later British rulers of India have employed the same policy of fostering divisions among the people, knowing well that divisions always weaken a nation and render it easier to hold in subjection.

Since the time of the early conquerors of India, this policy has been kept as much as possible out of sight; and sometimes it has been denied; and yet not infrequently eminent officials have been frank enough boldly to declare and defend it. As early as 1821, a British official, signing himself "Carnaticus," wrote in the *Asiatic Review* of May of that year:

Divide et Impera should be the motto of our Indian administration, whether political, civil or military.

About the time of the Mutiny, Lieutenant Colonel John Coke, Commandant at Moradabad, wrote:

Our endeavor should be to uphold in full force the (for us fortunate) separation which exists between the different religions and races, not to endeavor to amalgamate them. *Divide et impera* should be the principle of Indian government. . . .

Sir John Strachey said:

The existence side by side of hostile creeds among the Indian people is one of the strong points in our political position in India. . . .

Of course, the question arose early with them, What particular division could be taken advantage of that would be likely to be most effective? The answer was not far to seek. Religious divisions generally strike deepest. Just as in Christian lands rulers have often availed themselves of the divisions of the people into Catholics and Protestants, arraying one of these religious communities against the other to serve their own political ends, so it was natural that the British in India should take advantage of the great and conspicuous religious division of the Indian people into Hindus and Moslems to serve their own British political ends. Perfect political unity between these two great communities would mean practically the unity of all India. But a united India would be a danger to British rule. . . .

The particular ways most employed by the British to keep the Hindus and Mohammedans apart have been, and are, two, namely, *favoritism shown by the Government to the Mohammedans,* which, of course, tends to create jealousy on the part of the Hindus, and therefore estrangement; and, of late years, *communal elections.*

The favoritism shown by the Government to the Moslems has taken many forms, and it has generally been hidden and elusive; but its existence has been, and is, unmistakable.

Ramsay MacDonald, in his *Awakening of India* (p. 283), calls sharp attention to the widespread

suspicion that sinister influences have been and are at work on the part of the Government; that Mohammedan leaders have been and are inspired by certain British officials, and that these officials have pulled and continue to pull wires at Simla and in London, and of malice aforethought sow discord between the Mohammedan and Hindu communities, by showing to the Mohammedans special favors. . . .

A year or two ago, Lord Olivier, who was Secretary of State for India in the first MacDonald Government, wrote a letter to the London *Times,* confessing in the plainest words this favoritism. He said:

No one with a close acquaintance with Indian affairs will be prepared to deny that on the whole there is a predominant bias in British officialdom in favor of the Moslem community, partly on the ground of closer sympathy but more largely as a make-weight against Hindu nationalism.

This statement made a great stir in London, and Lord Olivier was widely censured. Much of the feeling was caused by what was regarded as his indiscretion in letting the public know something which the Government thought should be kept secret. . . .

Passing to the Communal Elections — the influence of these in estranging different sections of the Indian people, especially Hindus and Moslems, is so obvious

that no one dares to deny it. Just what are the Communal Elections? The plan of these, or to employ another name, the plan of Communal Representation, is a scheme by which men are elected to office not to represent the people as a whole, but a section of the people, a class, a division, especially a religious sect. The electorates are divided into compartments, so to speak, social, racial and religious; that is, the people who vote do not vote all together, as citizens all on an equality, and for representatives to represent them all as Indians, without reference to their social status or their religious faith, as is the case in this country and Canada and England and nearly all other countries. Instead of that, the members of different religious faiths, and different social classes, and different races, vote separately, and for candidates to represent them as belonging to separate and distinct faiths and classes and races.

For example the Bengal legislature of one hundred thirteen members has not been elected and does not exist as a legislative body of one hundred thirteen *Indians,* representing all the people of Bengal, or all the people of this, that and the other *district* of Bengal. On the contrary, forty-six members of the Legislature have been elected as Hindus to represent Hindus; thirty-eight as Mohammedans to represent Mohammedans; sixteen as Europeans to represent the relatively very small number of Europeans; two as Eurasians or Anglo-Indians to represent that section of the people; five as landholders, etc., etc. Of course the effect of such a dividing political system, of such a broken-up elective and representative plan, is in the greatest possible degree to destroy all feelings of citizenship, to crush out all patriotism, to prevent all interest in India as such or Bengal as such, and to destroy all care or concern for measures aiming to promote the benefit of the nation, the province or the city. Its effect is to cause each voter to concentrate his interest on the narrow and selfish affairs of his own particular class or race or religion. Could human ingenuity devise a political system in its very nature more certain to produce political, social and religious divisions and antagonisms, or better calculated to make religious, social and political unity in India impossible? . . .

Do the Indian people want the Communal system? The answer is, a few do. Extreme partisans, and narrow-minded sectarians, whether Hindus or Mohammedans, do; and extremely selfish men who care for nobody but themselves, and for no interests but their own or those of their own sect or class or party, these do. But these do not constitute the great body of the Indian people, nor include the ablest and most trusted leaders. The Hindus, who constitute more than two-thirds of the population of the nation, are against it almost to a man. The three or four millions of native Christians are the same. The more intelligent, more progressive and better element among the Mohammedans are against it. Who is responsible for this system?

Of course, the Government is. The Government created it, and insists on keeping it. . . .

The Indian Messenger (Calcutta) of May 20, 1926, also lays the responsibility for Communal electorates or Communal representation in India primarily upon Lord Minto. It says: "British imperialism has never failed to do all in its power to keep India divided, by pitting minorities against majorities; and in this way making British interests safe and secure." In this connection it quotes Lord Minto as saying: I am firmly convinced that any electoral representations in India would be doomed to mischievous failure which aimed at granting a personal enfranchisement regardless of the *beliefs* and *traditions* of the *communities* composing the population of this continent. . . .

Colonel Josiah Wedgwood, M.P., declares that the minds of those who formed the present Constitution of India (the Government of India Bill of 1919 — Dyarchy) were so full of the idea of Communal Elections that "the very thought of *India* vanished from the Bill, to be replaced by consideration for the separate communities of Hindu, Mohammedan, Sikh, Mahratta, non-Brahmin, Indian Christian, Anglo-Indian and English" — that is to say, representatives to the Assemblies and elsewhere were to be elected, not as Indians . . . and not to serve India, their common country, but to serve primarily their own *particular classes and religious sects*. . . .

As Mr. Lajpat Rai has pointed out, an absolutely clear proof . . . that the British find in the plan of communal electorates an effective means of keeping India divided and therefore of making their own mastery of her secure, is seen in the fact that this plan receives the enthusiastic support of the British press of India and the Tory press of Great Britain — in other words, of all parties that want to strengthen Britain's hold on India. . . .

Although the communal election scheme is so shaped as on the whole to favor the Mohammedans above the Hindus, it is well known . . . that by no means all the Mohammedans "bite at the bait" (of excessive offices and other favors) which the British Government holds out to them. . . .

The Honorable Syed Sirdar Ali Khan of Hyderabad, says in *The Times* of August 1, 1925:

No sane Mohammedan wants communal differences to be perpetuated. We want them to be eliminated. . . . The great majority of us trust that by co-operation of Moslems and Hindus we may attain self-government that will be not a Hindu government, but a government that will really represent India and will give to the Mohammedans that share in assisting the well-ordered progress of the country which they deserve by their numbers, their merits and their traditions. . . .

Do the British officials really want to stop the riots? Many of the Indian people find themselves compelled to believe that they do not; they say, "If they *wanted* to stop them, they *would* stop them; for they have the power." Not a few Indians believe that the British regard the riots as a valuable asset — as one of the best excuses they have for staying in India. . . .

They can get rid of the riots, and other forms of dangerous hostility, in one way and only one. And that is by ceasing to show favoritism to the Mohammedans or to any other community or party; and by giving to India electorates and elections so planned as to *unite* the people and cause them all to vote together as *citizens* of a *common country,* and in the *interest* of their *common country,* instead of electorates and elections planned in their very nature to *divide* the people, by setting them to voting as *Moslems,* as *Hindus,* as *Parsis,* as *Sikhs,* as *Christians,* and the *rest,* in the *interest of their rival sects.*

There is absolutely nothing fundamentally antagonistic between the Hindus and Mohammedans of India. They have lived together for more than seven hundred years, and are living together happily now in essentially every respect except as stirred to rivalries, jealousies and temporary hostilities by the presence and plannings of a foreign government, whose constant policy is that of the old Romans, *divide et impera.*

Hindu-Muslim Relations: The Congress View

JAWAHARLAL NEHRU

In the following selections from The Discovery of India *and* Toward Freedom *Jawaharlal Nehru provides a very different interpretation of the growing communal problem from that given in previous readings. His insistence that there were no fundamental divergences between Hindus and Muslims is of great importance for understanding how Indians, in contrast to Pakistanis, interpret the course of modern Indian history. Nehru paints an unflattering picture of Jinnah, depicting him as a leader unaware of the problems of the age and acting as the instrument of privilege and reaction.*

AFTER the Mutiny, the Indian Moslems had hesitated which way to turn. The British government had deliberately repressed them to an even greater degree than it had repressed the Hindus, and this repression had especially affected those sections of the Moslems from which the new middle class, the bourgeoisie, might have been drawn. They felt down and out and were intensely anti-British as well as conservative. British policy toward them underwent a gradual change in the seventies and became more favorable. This change was essentially due to the policy of balance and counterpoise which the British government consistently pursued. Still, in this process Sir Seyed Áhmad Khan played an important part. He was convinced that he could only raise the Moslems through cooperation with the British authorities. He was anxious to make them accept English education and thus to draw them out of their conservative shells. He had been much impressed by what he had seen of European civilization, and indeed some of his letters from Europe indicate that he was so dazed that he had rather lost his balance.

Sir Seyed was an ardent reformer, and he wanted to reconcile modern scientific thought with Islam. This was to be done, of course, not by attacking any basic belief but by a rationalistic interpretation of scripture. He pointed out the basic similarities between Islam and Christianity. He attacked purdah, the seclusion of women, among the Moslems. He was opposed to any allegiance to the Turkish khilafat. Above all, he was anxious to push a new type of education. The beginnings of the national movement frightened him, for he thought that any opposition to the British authorities would deprive him of their help in his educational program. That help appeared to him to be essential, so he tried to tone down anti-British sentiments among the Moslems and to turn away from the National Congress which was taking shape then. One of the declared objects of the

From Jawaharlal Nehru, *The Discovery of India* (New York, 1946), pp. 346–347, 350, 353–354, 356–358, 386, 389–399, and *Toward Freedom* (New York, 1941; published in Britain under the title *Autobiography*), pp. 385, 411. Selections from *The Discovery of India* reprinted by permission of The John Day Company, Inc., Asia Publishing House, and Mrs. Indira Nehru-Gandhi; selections from *Toward Freedom* reprinted by permission of The John Day Company, Inc., and The Bodley Head.

Aligarh College he founded was "to make the Mussalmans of India worthy and useful subjects of the British Crown." He was not opposed to the National Congress because he considered it predominantly a Hindu organization; he opposed it because he thought it was politically too aggressive (though it was mild enough in those days), and he wanted British help and cooperation. He tried to show that Moslems as a whole had not rebelled during the Mutiny and that many had remained loyal to the British power. He was in no way anti-Hindu or communally separatist. Repeatedly he emphasized that religious differences should have no political or national significance. "Do you not inhabit the same land?" he said. "Remember that the words Hindu and Muhomedan are only meant for religious distinction — otherwise all persons, whether Hindu or Mohammedan, even the Christians who reside in this country are all in this respect belonging to one and the same nation."

Sir Seyed Ahmad Khan's influence was confined to certain sections of the upper classes among the Moslems; he did not touch the urban or the rural masses. These masses were almost completely cut off from their upper classes and were far nearer to the Hindu masses. While some among the Moslem upper classes were descendants of the ruling groups during Moghul times, the masses had no such background or tradition. Most of them had been converted from the lowest strata of Hindu society and were most unhappily situated, being among the poorest and the most exploited. . . .

Sir Seyed succeeded in so far as the beginnings of English education among the Moslems were concerned, and in diverting the Moslem mind from the political movement. A Mohammedan educational conference was started, and this attracted the rising Moslem middle class in the professions and services.

None the less many prominent Moslems joined the National Congress. British policy became definitely pro-Moslem, or rather in favor of those elements among the Moslems who were opposed to the national movement. But early in the twentieth century the tendency toward nationalism and political activity became more noticeable among the younger generation of Moslems. To divert this and provide a safe channel for it, the Moslem League was started in 1906 under the inspiration of the British government and the leadership of one of its chief supporters, the Aga Khan. The League had two principal objects: loyalty to the British government and the safeguarding of Moslem interests. . . .

Though the mentality of the Moslem masses and the new growing middle class was shaped essentially by events, Sir Mohamad Iqbal played an important part in influencing the latter and especially the younger generation. The masses were hardly affected by him. Iqbal had begun by writing powerful nationalist poems in Urdu which had become popular . . . he was very far from being a mass leader; he was a poet, an intellectual, and a philosopher with affiliations to the old feudal order; he came from Kashmiri Brahman stock. He supplied in fine poetry, which was written in both Persian and Urdu, a philosophic background to the Moslem intelligentsia and thus diverted its mind in a separatist direction. His popularity was no doubt due to the quality of his poetry, but even more it was due to his having fulfilled a need when the Moslem mind was searching for some anchor to hold on to. The old pan-Islamic ideal had ceased to have any meaning; there was no khilafat and every Islamic country, Turkey most of all, was intensely nationalist, caring little for other Islamic peoples. Nationalism was in fact the dominant force in Asia as elsewhere, and in India the nationalist movement had grown powerful and challenged British rule repeatedly. That nationalism had a strong appeal to the Moslem mind in India, and large numbers of Moslems had played a leading part in its struggle for freedom. Yet Indian nationalism was dominated by Hindus and had a hinduized look. So a conflict arose in the Moslem mind; many accepted that nationalism, trying to influence it in the direction of their choice; many sympathized with it and yet remained aloof, uncertain; and yet many others began to drift in a separatist direction for which Iqbal's poetic and philosophic approach had prepared them.

This, I imagine, was the background out of which, in recent years, arose the cry for a division of India. There were many reasons, many contributory causes, errors and mistakes on every side, and especially the deliberate separatist policy of the British government. But behind all these was this psychological background which itself was produced, apart from certain historical causes, by the delay in the development of a Moslem middle class in India. Essentially the internal conflict in India, apart from the nationalist struggle against foreign domination, is between the remnants of the feudal order and modernist ideas and institutions. That conflict exists on the national plane as well as within each major group, Hindu, Moslem, and others. The national movement, as represented essentially by the National Congress, undoubtedly represents the historic process of growth toward these new ideas and institutions, though it tries to adapt these to some of the old foundations. Because of this, it has attracted to its fold all manner of people differing widely among themselves. On the Hindu side, an exclusive and rigid social order has come in the way of growth, and what is more, frightened other groups. But this social order itself has been undermined and is fast losing its rigidity, and in any event is not strong enough to obstruct the growth of the national movement in its widest political and social sense, which has developed enough impetus to go ahead in spite of obstacles. On the Moslem side, feudal elements have continued to be strong and have succeeded in imposing their leadership on their masses. There has been a difference of a generation or more in the development of the Hindu and Moslem middle classes, and that difference continues to show itself in

many directions, political, economic, and other. It is this lag which produces a psychology of fear among the Moslems.

Pakistan, the proposal to divide India, however much it may appeal emotionally to some, is of course no solution for this backwardness, and it is much more likely to strengthen the hold of feudal elements for some more time and delay the economic progress of the Moslems. Iqbal was one of the early advocates of Pakistan, and yet he appears to have realized its inherent danger and absurdity. . . .

Moslem young men were . . . being affected by . . . revolutionary ideas. The Aligarh College had tried to check these tendencies, and now, under government inspiration, the Aga Khan and others started the Moslem League to provide a political platform for Moslems and thus keep them away from Congress. More important still, and of vital significance to India's future development, it was decided to introduce separate electorates for Moslems. Henceforward Moslems could only stand for election and be elected by separate Moslem electorates. A political barrier was created around them, isolating them from the rest of India and reversing the unifying and amalgamating process which had been going on for centuries and which was inevitably being speeded up by technological developments. This barrier was a small one at first, for the electorates were very limited, but with every extension of the franchise it grew and affected the whole structure of public and social life, like some canker which corrupted the entire system. It poisoned municipal and local self-government and ultimately it led to fantastic divisions. There came into existence (much later) separate Moslem trade unions and students' organizations and merchants' chambers. Because the Moslems were backward in all these activities, these organizations were not real organic growths from below but were artificially created from above, and their leadership was held by the old semifeudal type of person. Thus, to some extent, the Moslem middle classes and even the masses were isolated from the currents of growth which were influencing the rest of India. There were vested interests enough in India created or preserved by the British government. Now an additional and powerful vested interest was created by separate electorates.

It was not a temporary evil which tended to fade away with a developing political consciousness. Nurtured by official policy, it grew and spread and obscured the real problems before the country, whether political, social, or economic. It created divisions and ill feeling where there had been none previously, and it actually weakened the favored group by increasing a tendency to depend on artificial props and not to think in terms of self-reliance. . . .

Separate electorates thus weakened the groups that were already weak or backward; they encouraged separatist tendencies and prevented the growth of national unity, they were the negation of democracy, they created new vested interests of the most reactionary kind, they lowered standards, and they diverted attention from the real economic problems of the country which were common to all. These electorates, first introduced among the Moslems, spread to other minorities and groups till India became a mosaic of these separate compartments. Possibly they may have done some good for a little while, though I am unable to spot it; but undoubtedly the injury they have caused to every department of Indian life has been prodigious. Out of them have grown all manner of separatist tendencies and finally the demand for a splitting up of India.

Lord Morley was the Secretary of State for India when these separate electorates were introduced. He resisted them, but ultimately agreed under pressure from the viceroy. He has pointed out in his diary the dangers inherent in such a method and how they would inevitably delay the development of representative institutions. Probably this was exactly what the viceroy and his colleagues intended. In the Montagu-Chelmsford Report on Indian Constitutional Reform (1918) the dangers of these communal electorates were again emphasized:

Division by creeds and classes means the creation of political camps organized against each other, and teaches men to think as partisans and not as citizens. . . . We regard any system of communal electorates, therefore, as a very serious hindrance to the development of the self-governing principle.

*   *   *

The communal problem, as it was called, was one of adjusting the claims of the minorities and giving them sufficient protection from majority action. Minorities in India, it must be remembered, are not racial or national minorities as in Europe; they are religious minorities. Racially India is a patchwork and a curious mixture, but no racial questions have arisen or can arise in India. Religion transcends these racial differences, which fade into one another and are often hard to distinguish. Religious barriers are obviously not permanent, as conversions can take place from one religion to another, and a person changing his religion does not thereby lose his racial background or his cultural and linguistic inheritance. Latterly religion in any real sense of the word, has played little part in Indian political conflicts, though the word is often enough used and exploited. Religious differences, as such, do not come in the way, for there is a great deal of mutual tolerance for them. In political matters, religion has been displaced by what is called communalism, a narrow group mentality basing itself on a religious community but in reality concerned with political power and patronage for the group concerned.

Repeated efforts were made by the Congress as well as other organizations to settle this communal problem with the consent of the various groups concerned. Some partial success was achieved, but there was always a basic difficulty — the presence and policy of the British government. Naturally the British did not favor any real settlement which would strengthen the political movement — now grown to mass proportions — against them. It was a triangle, with the government in a position to play off one side against the other by giving special privileges. If the other parties had been wise enough, they could have overcome even this obstacle; but they lacked wisdom and foresight. Whenever a settlement was almost reached, the government would take some step which upset the balance.

*   *   *

The Congress organization is certainly one of the most democratic that I know of anywhere in the world, both in theory and practice. Through its tens of thousands of local committees spread out all over the country it had trained the people in democratic ways and achieved striking success in this. The fact that a dominating and very popular personality like Gandhi was connected with it did not lessen that essential democracy of the Congress. In times of crisis and struggle there was an inevitable tendency to look to the leader for guidance, as in every country, and such crises were frequent. Nothing is more absurd than to call the Congress an authoritarian organization, and it is interesting to note that such charges are usually made by high representatives of British authority, which is the essence of authoritarianism in India. . . .

We failed in finding a solution for the communal problem agreeable to all parties concerned, and certainly we must share the blame as we have to shoulder the consequences for this failure. But how does one get everybody to agree to any important proposition or change? There are always feudal and reactionary elements who are opposed to all change, and there are those who want political, economic, and social change. When it is the policy of the ruling power to set up such groups and encourage them, even though they might represent an infinitesimal proportion of the population, then change can only come through successful revolution. It is obvious that there are any number of feudal and reactionary groups in India, some native to the soil and some created and nurtured by the British. In numbers they may be small, but they have the backing of the British power. . . .

The chief Hindu communal organization is the Hindu Mahasabha, the counterpart of the Moslem League, but relatively less important. It is as aggressively communal as the League, but it tries to cover up its extreme narrowness of outlook by using some kind of vague national terminology, though its outlook is more revivalist than progressive. It is peculiarly unfortunate in some of its leaders who indulge in irresponsible and violent diatribes, as indeed some of the Moslem League leaders also do. This verbal warfare, indulged in on both sides, is a constant irritant. It takes the place of action.

The Moslem League's communal attitude was often difficult and unreasonable in the past, but no less unreasonable was the attitude of the Hindu Mahasabha. The Hindu minorities in the Punjab and Sind, and the dominant Sikh group in the Punjab, were often obstructive and came in the way of settlement. British policy was to encourage and emphasize these differences and to give importance to communal organizations as against the Congress.

One test of the importance of a group or party, or at any rate of its hold on the people, is an election. During the general elections in India in 1937 the Hindu Mahasabha failed completely; it was nowhere in the picture. The Moslem League did better, but on the whole its showing was poor, especially in the predominantly Moslem provinces. In the Punjab and Sind it failed completely, in Bengal it met with only partial success. In the North-West Frontier Province, Congress formed a ministry later. In the Moslem minority provinces the League met with greater success on the whole, but there were also independent Moslem groups as well as Moslems elected as Congressmen.

Then began a remarkable campaign on behalf of the Moslem League against the

Congress governments in the provinces and the Congress organization itself. Day after day it was repeated that these governments were committing "atrocities" on the Moslems. Those governments contained Moslem ministers also, but they were not members of the Moslem League. What these "atrocities" were it was not usually stated; or some petty local incidents, which had nothing to do with the government, were distorted and magnified. Some minor errors of some departments, which were soon rectified, became "atrocities." Sometimes entirely false and baseless charges were made. Even a report was issued, fantastic in its contents and having little to do with any facts. Congress governments invited those who made the charges to supply particulars for investigation or to come and inquire themselves with government help. No one took advantage of these offers. . . .

I had made a close study of nazi methods of propaganda since Hitler's rise to power, and I was astonished to find something very similar taking place in India. A year later, in 1938, when Czechoslovakia had to face the Sudetenland crisis, the nazi methods employed there were studied and referred to with approval by Moslem League spokesmen. A comparison was drawn between the position of Sudetenland Germans and Indian Moslems. Violence and incitements in speeches and in some newspapers became marked. A Congress Moslem minister was stabbed, and there was no condemnation of this from any Moslem League leader; in fact it was condoned. Other exhibitions of violence frequently took place.

I was terribly depressed by these developments and by the general lowering of the standards of public life. Violence, vulgarity, and irresponsibility were on the increase, and it appeared that they were approved of by responsible leaders of the Moslem League. . . . There was a regular rampage on the part of members or sympathizers of the Moslem League to make the Moslem masses believe that something terrible was happening and that the Congress was to blame. What that terrible thing was nobody seemed to know. But surely there must be something behind all this shouting and cursing, if not here then elsewhere. During by-elections the cry raised was "Islam in danger," and voters were asked to take their oaths on the holy book to vote for the Moslem League candidate.

. . . for the first time in its history the Moslem League got a mass backing and began to develop into a mass organization. Much as I regretted what was happening, I welcomed this development in a way, as I thought that this might lead ultimately to a change in the feudal leadership and more progressive elements would come forward. The real difficulty thus far had been the extreme political and social backwardness of the Moslems, which made them liable to exploitation by reactionary leaders.

Mr. M. A. Jinnah himself was more advanced than most of his colleagues of the Moslem League. Indeed he stood head and shoulders above them and had therefore become the indispensable leader. From public platforms he confessed his great dissatisfaction with the opportunism, and even worse failings, of his colleagues. He knew well that a great part of the advanced, selfless, and courageous element among the Moslems had joined and worked with the Congress. And yet some destiny or course of events had thrown him among the very people for whom he had no respect. He was their leader, but he could only keep them together by becoming himself a prisoner to their reactionary ideologies. Not that he was an unwilling prisoner, so far as the ideologies were concerned, for despite his external modernism, he belonged to an older generation which was hardly aware of modern political thought or developments. Of economics, which overshadow the world today, he appeared to be entirely ignorant. The extraordinary occurrences that had taken place all over the world since World War I had apparently had no effect on him. He had left the Congress when that organization had taken a political leap forward. The gap had widened as the Congress developed an economic and mass outlook. But Mr. Jinnah seemed to have remained ideologically in that identical place where he stood a generation ago, or rather he had gone further back, for now he condemned both India's unity and democracy. . . .

When I was Congress president, I wrote to Mr. Jinnah on several occasions and requested him to tell us exactly what he would like us to do. I asked him what the League wanted and what its definite objectives were. I also wanted to know what the grievances of the League were against the Congress governments. The idea was that we might clarify matters by correspondence and then discuss personally the important points that had risen in it. Mr. Jinnah sent me long replies but failed to enlighten me. It was extraordinary how he avoided telling me, or anyone else, exactly what he wanted or what the grievances of the League were. . . .

Subsequently Gandhiji and others met Mr. Jinnah several times. They talked for hours but never got beyond a preliminary stage. Our proposal was that representatives of the Congress and the League should meet and discuss all their mutual problems. Mr. Jinnah said that this could only be done after we recognized publicly that the Moslem League was the sole representative organization of the Moslems of India, and the Congress should consider itself a purely Hindu organization. This created an obvious difficulty. We recognized, of course, the importance of the League, and because of that we had approached it. But how could we ignore many other Moslem organizations, some closely associated with us? Also there were large numbers of Moslems in the Congress itself and among our highest executives. To admit Mr. Jinnah's claim meant in effect to push out our old Moslem colleagues from the Congress, and declare that the Congress was not open to them. It was to change the fundamental character of the Congress, and from a national organization, open to all, convert it into a communal body. That was inconceivable for us.

If the Congress had not already been there, we would have had to build up a new national organization open to every Indian. . . .

Mr. Jinnah's demand was based on a new theory he had recently propounded — that India consisted of two nations, Hindu and Moslem. Why only two I do not know, for if nationality was based on religion, then there were many nations in India. Of two brothers one may be a Hindu, another a Moslem; they would belong to two different nations. These two nations existed in varying proportions in most of the villages of India. They were nations which had no boundaries; they overlapped. A Bengali Moslem and a Bengali Hindu, living together, speaking the same language and having much the same traditions and customs, belonged to different nations. All this was very difficult to grasp; it seemed a reversion to some medieval theory. . . .

From Mr. Jinnah's two-nation theory developed the conception of Pakistan, or splitting up India. That of course did not solve the problem of the two "nations" for they were all over the place. But that gave body to a metaphysical conception. . . .

The Congress represented not only the nationalist urge of India, which had grown with the growth of the new bourgeoisie, but also, to a large extent, proletarian urges for social change. This sometimes produced inner conflicts within Congress, and the landlord class and the big industrialists, though often nationalistic, kept aloof from it for fear of socialistic changes. Within the Congress, socialists and communists found a place and could influence Congress policy. The communal organizations, whether Hindu or Moslem, were closely associated with the feudal and conservative elements and were opposed to any revolutionary social change. The real conflict had, therefore, nothing to do with religion, though religion often masked the issue, but was essentially between those who stood for a nationalist-democratic-socially revolutionary policy and those who were concerned with preserving the relics of a feudal regime. In a crisis, the latter inevitably depend upon foreign support which is interested in preserving the status quo.

*   *   *

Let us be clear about it. This communal question is essentially one of protection of vested interests, and religion has always been a useful stalking horse for this purpose. Those who have feudal privileges and vested interests fear change and become the camp followers of British imperialism. The British Government, on the other hand, delight in using the communal argument to deny freedom, democracy, or any major change, and to hold on to power and privilege in India. That is the *raison d'être* and the justification of communalism in India. . . .

I am afraid I cannot get excited over this communal issue, important as it is temporarily. It is, after all, a side issue, and it can have no real importance in the larger scheme of things. Those who think of it as the major issue think in terms of British imperialism continuing permanently in this country. Without that basis of thought, they would not attach so much importance to one of its inevitable offshoots. I have no such fear, and so my vision of a future India contains neither imperialism nor communalism.

The Congress Ministries and the League

SIR REGINALD COUPLAND

Sir Reginald Coupland, Beit Professor of Colonial History in Oxford University, was one of the foremost historians of Britain's imperial policies in Africa and India. In the following selection he argues that the authoritarian nature of the Congress helped to make a rapprochement with the Muslim League impossible.

. . . The political philosophy of the Congress is unitarian. Its own organization . . . is highly centralised. . . . Pandit Nehru gave a new interpretation to the principle of responsible government.

It is to the Congress as a whole that the electorate gave allegiance, and it is the Congress that is responsible to the electorate. The Ministers and the Congress Parties in the Legislatures are responsible to the Congress and only through it to the electorate.

In pursuance of this doctrine, from the day they took office to the day they resigned (1937–1939), the Congress Ministries were firmly subjected to "Central" control; and the Congress members of the Legislatures were under the same "high command," not only in the Congress Provinces but also in those in which they were a minority. This did not mean that the conduct of Congress politicians in any Province ran counter to the public opinion of their constituencies; but it did mean that their conduct was not determined by that public opinion but by the orders of the Congress "Centre.". . .

It was not only the Working Committee's control of the Congress Ministries that showed that a "Congress Raj" had been established in their Provinces. It was betrayed by the conduct and bearing of Congressmen, both in the performance of public duties and as individuals, at the outset of the new regime. *Bande Mataram* was sung to open proceedings in the Provincial Legislatures. The tricolour (Congress) was hoisted over local administrative buildings. And, not unnaturally, all the subordinate branches of the "parallel" Government now felt themselves authorised to govern. Congress Committees issued orders. In some districts Congress police stations were opened and Congress police began to investigate crime. More disquieting to those who remembered the part played by paramilitary formations in Europe, the United Provinces Provincial Committee set up a "Military Department" and declared its intention of raising a Provincial force 500,-000 strong to be brigaded with other Provincial forces in a great "National Army." . . . A less sinister phenomenon, but one which made a deep impression on the minorities, was the demeanour of the rank and file of Congressmen, especially the younger ones, on the morrow of their electoral victory. Many of them behaved as if they were a ruling caste, as if they owned the country. . . .

From Sir Reginald Coupland, *India, A Re-statement* (London, 1945), pp. 170–171, 174–176, 180–182. Reprinted by permission of Oxford University Press.

These tendencies were checked as time went on. . . . But the harm had been done. All the people of the Congress Provinces who were not Congressmen — and they numbered many millions — had been quick to observe the Congress' disclosure of what can only be called a totalitarian mentality. That word has an ugly sound, and Congress methods, it need hardly be said, are not those of Axis barbarism. Other parties are not suppressed. Opinion is free. Opposition within the Congress ranks to the will of its "high command" is disciplined indeed, but at the worst by no more than expulsion from the party. The conduct of the Congress can no more be likened to that of the Nazi and Fascist parties than the character of Mr. Gandhi can be likened to that of the Axis dictators. But the essence of totalitarianism is not in its methods but in its principle, and its principle is simply one-party government or the identification of the Party with the State. . . .

It is the Moslems, now numbering about 100 millions, who have always been the major crux. But in 1937 the political organization of the community was still relatively backward. True, the great majority of the Moslem seats at the elections were won by non-Congress Moslems; but they were candidates of various local parties: there was no common Moslem front. The League was the strongest party in the Hindu-majority Provinces; but it was still mainly composed of upper-class politicians, its membership was relatively small, it had little contact with the Moslem masses; and in the Moslem-majority Provinces its position was even weaker. It was little known on the Frontier. In the Punjab it was overshadowed by the Unionist Party. Neither in Bengal nor in Sind had it won a majority of Moslem votes. Nevertheless its mere existence invalidated the Congress claim to speak for all Indian Moslems who desired the freedom of India.

In this situation two choices were open to the Congress leaders after their victory at the polls. One was to take the League into partnership, to constitute Congress-League Coalition Ministries in the Congress-majority Provinces. This is what Mr. Jinnah had plainly suggested before the elections, and what was definitely expected in the U.P. (United Provinces) where the League was the strongest. To politicians schooled in the British parliamentary tradition this choice might well have seemed attractive: the morrow of a victory, it might have been thought, was the time for compromise and conciliation. But the Congress leaders took the other path. They decided not to come to terms with the League but to override it and try to absorb it.

. . . the Congress leaders put into operation a twofold policy. First, the leaders of the League in the U.P. — and the decision made there applied to the other "Congress Provinces" — were plainly told there would be no coalition. One or two of them might become Ministers, but only if they became Congressmen. The League group in the Legislature must: "cease to function as a separate group"; it must be merged in the Congress Party; and its members must accept the majority decisions of the Party like any other members. Since the Congress seemed assured of an electoral majority in most, if not all, of these Provinces for an indefinite time to come, the choice thus presented to the League leaders was hard. They must either dissolve the League and be absorbed in an organisation which, though non-communal in principle, was overwhelmingly Hindu in personnel, or lose all chance of office in their Provincial Government for as long ahead as they could see.

Secondly, the Congress launched what was known as a "mass-contact" movement among the scattered Moslem country-folk. They were told that the Congress victory implied no threat to their religion; for the Congress was non-communal and had repeatedly pledged itself to safeguard the rights of all communities. The real issue was not communal but economic, and the Congress, not the League, was the champion of the poor and had put in hand a drastic policy of agrarian reform which would benefit Moslem peasants equally with Hindu. Let them, therefore, strengthen the hands of the Congress in its task of social uplift by joining those many Moslems who had been members of the Party since its birth.

. . . this attempt to coerce the League was an unqualified failure. The Moslem reaction . . . marks an historic turning-point in the course of Indian politics.

Gandhi's Role

R. C. MAJUMDAR

Mahatma Gandhi sought to heal the Hindu-Muslim breach, but according to some scholars, his efforts worsened relations. R. C. Majumdar, one of India's most eminent historians and a persistent critic of what he regards as attempts to falsify history to serve nationalist ends, presents such a view in the following selection. Dr. Majumdar is the editor of the monumental *History and Culture of the Indian People,* of which seven volumes have been published, and the author of many historical studies, including the controversial *History of the Freedom Movement in India* in three volumes.

THE pan-Islamic movement gathered force at the end of the first World War. The Muslims of India regarded the treatment of Turkey as a great betrayal on the part of the British and a storm of indignation broke out among them. When prayers and deputations to the Government failed to achieve any modification of the terms of the treaty imposed upon Turkey, the Indian Muslims started a vigorous agitation to bring pressure upon Britain to change her policy towards Turkey. It was in connection with this agitation — known as the Khilafat agitation — that Gandhi came to play a leading part in Indian politics. Gandhi's handling of the Hindu-Muslim problem profoundly affected the course of struggle for independence. His anxiety for the Hindu-Muslim unity deserves all praise, but his was a sentimental approach to the problem and was not based on a realistic appreciation of the situation. He perhaps thought that by the magic of his non-violence he would provide synthesis where none appeared possible. He does not appear to have understood the fundamental differences that separated the Muslims from the Hindus, and were too deep to be healed merely by slogans of friendship and fraternity. He failed to understand the real cause of tension between the two communities, because he did not study the problem in its true historical perspective. He shared the common views of the Hindu political leaders that the communalistic outlook of the Muslims blocked the progress of Indian nationalism which they held out as a great and noble ideal. But the Hindus forgot that while it is easy to follow a noble ideal when it also subserves your material interest, it is more difficult to accept it when, instead, it involves sacrifice and sufferings. Independence of India would give the majority community all the power and prestige, and the minority would be at their mercy. The Muslims could not forget that not long ago they were masters of the Hindus. To be subject to the British was bad enough, but subjection to Hindu domination would be far worse. Such a mentality may be regarded as ignoble from the higher standpoint of nationality, but it is difficult to say that it is unnatural. The Hindu leaders, however, conveniently ignored this point of view altogether. Like them Gandhi also believed that most of the

From R. C. Majumdar, *Three Phases of the Freedom Movement* (Bombay, 1961), pp. 47–52. Reprinted by permission of Bharatiya Vidya Bhavan.

Muslim leaders were inspired by the lofty sentiments of nationalism. Muhammad Ali, whom he called his "dear brother," was one of the greatest nationalist Muslims in his opinion, and for his sake alone he rejected a golden opportunity to come to terms with the British during the visit of the Prince of Wales in 1921. But Muhammad Ali gave an admirable exposition of the real Muslim view in his famous article, entitled the "Communal Patriots," written in 1912:

The Hindu communal patriot . . . sprang into existence with Swaraj as his war-cry. He refuses to give quarter to the Muslim unless the latter quietly shuffles off his individuality and becomes completely Hinduized. He knows, of course, the use of the words like "India" and "territorial nationality", and they form an important part of his vocabulary. But the Muslims weigh on his consciousness all the same, as a troublesome irrelevance; and he would thank his stars if some great exodus or even a geological cataclysm could give him riddance.

As in 1912, so again in 1918, resentment against the British for their treatment of Turkey once more drew the Indian Muslims towards the Hindus. Muhammad Ali, who had openly proclaimed that he was a Muslim first and an Indian afterwards, sought for the help and support of Gandhi in this crisis for Turkey, and Gandhi readily agreed. Whatever one might think of his decision to take the leadership in a campaign with which India had no direct concern, his approach to the Khilafat question certainly appears to be very puzzling, not to put it more bluntly.

In his letter to the Viceroy he wrote that the safety of the British Empire depends upon the just treatment of the Khilafatist demand and of the Indians' claim to Home Rule. In other words, he attached equal importance to the independence of India and satisfaction of the claims of Indian Muslims regarding the integrity of the Khilafat in Turkey. Nay, more, he even gave priority to Muslim claim; for he invoked his *Brahmastra,* or the most potent

weapon, namely Satyagraha, for the first time, not for the Home Rule of India, nor for the redress of Punjab atrocities, but for enforcing the Muslim demands, the other two items being added later, on second and third thoughts. If we remember that no other Muslim country in the world was prepared to sacrifice an iota of its national interest for the sake of Khilafat, and that Turkey herself a few years later abolished the Khilafat as a useless appendage to Turkish sovereignty, Gandhi's backing of the Muslim claim, even to the extent of giving it priority over Home Rule, baffles all rational explanation.

Gandhi is reported to have said, in his justification, that such a chance of winning over the Muslims would never come in a hundred years' time. This does little credit either to the head or heart of Gandhi. To seriously think that the policy of a European coalition towards Turkey could be modified by Satyagraha in India, implies ignorance of European politics, though some would like to call it "a rare sense of expediency sharpened by a sense of his own apostolic power." An alternative hypothesis is to suppose that Gandhi deliberately encouraged the Muslims in a fruitless and hopeless task for the sake of promoting the political interests of the Hindus. But such an attitude is unthinkable in the case of Gandhi. It has been suggested by some that "Gandhi was always capable of working himself up to a Messianic zeal, as an instrument of God; and in such cases Messianic zeal is known to be harnessed to a desire to work miracles." Miracles may happen in the world. But they do not constitute a proper subject of historical inquiry, and should not form the basis of political judgment.

Further, to believe that any effort to help the Muslims on this occasion would for ever secure the Hindu-Muslim unity, only betrays a lack of full knowledge regarding the growth of Muslim nationalism sketched above. Gandhi was not disillusioned even by the article of his "dear brother" Muhammad Ali, referred to above. Muhammad

Ali laughed at the idea that the Muslims would make matters up with the Hindus because something happened to Muslims outside India, and very pertinently asked, "Have the questions that really divide the two communities lost their force and meaning? If not, then the problem remains exactly where it was at any time in recent Indian history." This is the realistic point of view. To think that a temporary palliative over a side-issue, having no relation with India, would solve the long-standing problem was an absurd idea, to say the least of it.

But there is a far more serious objection to Gandhi's policy. Howsoever opinions might differ as to the basic elements that constitute a nationality, there is a consensus of opinion in one respect. Different groups of people living together cannot constitute a nation unless they have common sympathy, agreement, and interest to an extent, such as does not subsist between any one of them and any nation outside these groups. If a hundred million Muslims in India feel more vitally interested in the welfare of Turkey and other Muslim States outside India, than that of India herself, they can hardly be regarded as a unit of Indian nation. Gandhi failed to realize that the pan-Islamic movement in India, which he chose to lead, cut at the very root of Indian nationality. By his own admission that the Khilafat question was a vital one for Indian Muslims, even more vital than Home Rule for India, Gandhi himself put a seal of approval to the oft-repeated claim of Indian Muslims that they formed a separate nation, that they were in India but not of India.

After having cut at the very root of Indian nationalism, by recognizing the Muslims, for all political purposes, as forming a separate nation, once in 1916, and again in 1919, Gandhi and his followers made a complete *volte-face* in 1937. When Jinnah, one of the few real nationalists among the Muslims at one time, suggested a coalition Ministry of the Congress and

the Muslim League, the Congress assumed a lofty tone of undiluted Indian nationalism, and refused to entertain any proposal that might have the appearance of representing the Muslims as a separate political unit. The Congress virtually refused to form a coalition ministry with the Muslims unless they liquidated the Muslim League and repudiated all vestiges of their claim to form a separate political entity. Nobody who had any knowledge of the background of Muslim politics could imagine for a moment that the Muslim League would commit political *Hara-kiri* at the bidding of the Congress.

It was a momentous decision, probably inspired by belated recognition of what true nationalism demands. But this sense dawned upon the Hindu leaders too late, and the decision of 1937 substantiated Muhammad Ali's charge against the Hindus, mentioned before. Gandhi fully justified the decision in an article published in the *Harijan* on 15 June, 1940. He maintained that there were only two parties in India, namely, those who support the Congress and those who do not, and then added that "between the two there is no meeting ground without the one or the other surrendering its purpose." Worse still, Gandhi declared: It is an illusion created by ourselves that we must come to an agreement with all parties, before we can make any progress. Gandhi thus slammed the door of negotiations in the face of Jinnah, though he later repeatedly tried in vain to open it again. Jinnah now finally realized that the Muslims, as a separate community, had no political prospects in India. They had no chance of sharing political power with the Hindus; they must either surrender their individuality or cut themselves adrift from the Hindus. The Congress ultimatum was thus the signal for the parting of the ways which, by inevitable stages, led to Pakistan. All proposals for amicable settlement on the basis of the partition of India were violently denounced, and Gandhi held to the last that the partition could only be effected over his dead body. But at last the doctrinaire yielded to the realist. Gandhi had evidently hoped against hope to work a miracle by his non-violence. But Jinnah's "Direct Action" proved a more effective weapon for achieving independence than Satyagraha. Violence triumphed over non-violence. . . .

Muslim Opposition to Pakistan

Z. H. FARUQI

For an understanding of the complexity of the argument over Partition, it is important to remember that a very important group of orthodox Muslims were violently opposed to the whole idea of a separate state for Muslims. Their arguments were very different from those of the leaders of the Indian National Congress. The spokesmen for this group were members of the Jamiyat-ul-Ulama-i-Hind, an organization of *ulama*, or learned Muslim scholars. They were associated with the famous school of Islamic learning at Deoband, ninety miles from Delhi, which had been established in 1867 to maintain the spirit of Islam against the encroachments of British rule. The reasons why the orthodox scholars of Deoband opposed the creation of Pakistan are given in this selection from a book on the movement by Z. H. Faruqi, Principal of the Jamia Millia Islami, a Muslim college in Delhi. The point of view of the Deoband school is to be distinguished from that of nationalist Muslims like Maulana Azad, whose support of a united India was based more on secular than on religious considerations.

THE Jam'iyat never conceded the doctrine of two nations as propounded by the League. Since its very inception it stood for a "United Indian Nationalism" ("muttahidah qawmīyat"). This formed the very core of all the League-Jam'iyat differences. The Jam'iyat's stand on this fundamental and controversial point was fully explained by Mawlānā Ḥusain Aḥmad Madanī, one of its chief spokesmen and for years its president, in his "Muttaḥidah Qawmīyat aur Islām" (Delhi, 1938) in the light of the Quranic verses and the Prophetic traditions. Again, in his presidential address at the annual session of the Jam'iyat-ul-'Ulamā' at Jaunpur (U.P.) in June, 1940, he declared:

We, the inhabitants of India, in so far as we are Indians, have one thing in common and that is our Indianness which remains unchanged in spite of our religious and cultural differences. As the diversities in our appearances, individual qualities and personal traits and colour and stature do not affect our common humanness, similarly our religious and cultural differences do not interfere with our common associations with our homeland. Therefore, like the other "millats" and non-Muslim religio-cultural groups, it is incumbent upon the Muslims to have concern with and struggle for the attainment of national interests and fight against the evils that hamper the country's progress and prosperity. . . . This duty which arises out of our common sharing in the happiness and misery of our motherland, is obligatory on all. Religious differences, in no case, serve as an impediment in the way of fulfilling this obligation. This is what I mean by the "muttaḥidah qawmīyat." The other meanings which the people are attributing to it are wrong and baseless. The Congress, having the same stand [as ours] has made provisions in its fundamentals for the protection of all religions, cultures and languages. The European con-

From Ziya-ul-Hasan Faruqi, *The Deoband School and the Demand for Pakistan* (Bombay, 1963), pp. 103–121. Reprinted by permission of Asia Publishing House.

ception of nationalism or the outlook of [certain] individual Congressmen regarding the different interpretations of the Congress fundamentals is unacceptable to the Jam'īyat. It denounces it and is totally opposed to it.

Out of this basic difference between the League and the Jam'īyat arose the latter's vehement opposition to the League's demand for the division of the country. Deoband became the citadel of this opposition as Aligarh, quite naturally, turned out to be the training centre of the "mujāhidīn-i-Pākistān." It is meaningful to note that the two major centres of Muslim education in India, representing, since their very beginning, the two different trends in the politico-intellectual life of the Indian Muslims, finally collided against each other in the moulding of the ultimate destiny of the Muslims in the Indian sub-continent. Deoband never succeeded in shaking off the suspicions it entertained about the pronounced cooperation of Aligarh with the British regime in India.

* * *

Rightly or wrongly, the Jam'īyat and the Deoband leadership, which considered the British Imperialism the greatest enemy of Islam and its followers, seriously suspected a British hand in the proposed scheme of the partition of the country and repeatedly warned the Muslims of the dangers involved in it. They also warned them that the scheme, if it materialized, would divide the Muslim community into three groups and would be more harmful to them than to any other community in the sub-continent; it would be still more ruinous to that group of Muslims who would be left behind in the Hindu provinces as a smaller and less effective minority. . . .

Extremely bewildered by the situation, the Jam'īyat warned the Muslims of the dangerous game the League was playing at a very high stake. Even as early as 1940 Mawlānā Muḥammad Sajjād of Bihar, one of the geniuses of the Jam'īyat-ul-'Ulamā', analysing the Lahore Resolution had remarked that there was nothing in it that

could give the least satisfaction to the Muslims living in the Hindu provinces; the Resolution was mainly related to the Muslims of those areas where they were already in a majority. He had recorded his astonishment at the suggestion that the strength of the Muslim provinces would be a guarantee for the safeguards of the Muslims living in the Hindu majority provinces. The same year Mawlānā Madanī characterized the Pakistan movement as the "death-knell for the Muslims of the areas where they were in a minority." In short, the Jam'īyat leaders were unable to understand the wisdom of the policy advocated by Mr. Jinnāh, viz., that "in order to liberate 7 crores of Muslims where they are in a majority he was willing to perform the last ceremony of martyrdom if necessary and let two crores of Muslims be smashed." They were also doubtful about the practicality of the idea embodied in his remark that "as a self-respecting people we in the Muslim minority provinces say boldly that we are prepared to undergo every suffering and sacrifice for the emancipation and liberation of our brethren in regions of Muslim majority. . . . *But the fact is that the creation of these independent states will be the surest guarantee for the fair treatment of the minorities.*" [Italics are ours.] They knew well that by this remark Mr. Jinnāh was pointing to the "balance theory," but they had their own misgivings on this point. They thought that separation was not necessary and could not be a sure guarantee for inculcating a sense of responsibility in the majority towards the minorities; indeed unity provided a more favourable atmosphere for the growth of this kind of responsibility. What they considered implied in the remark was the sense of fear in the majority in one state of retaliation by another majority in the other state; in other words, minorities were to be doomed to remain as hostages in their respective states. They regarded this position not only as dubious but as foolish and mad. . . .

The Deoband leadership opposed the de-

mand for Pakistan also from the viewpoint
of the difficulties its realization would involve in the missionary activities of the
Muslims. As stated in the previous chapter,
it was one of the objectives of the Jam'īyat-
ul-'Ulamā' to propagate and spread Islam
through peaceful missionary work. The atmosphere of hatred and antagonism that
surrounded the Indian politics in the wake
of the growing popularity of the League
demand for a separate homeland, thought
the 'ulamā', would hamper the progress of
Islam as such and put great obstacles in the
way of missionary work. Their contention
was that Islam was a proselytizing religion
and needed for its spread an atmosphere
of love, peace and harmony. Since the very
beginning they were alarmed at the spreading tide of communal hatred in the country
and were trying their best to check it. They
knew that it was not only the Muslims
who were responsible for this sorry state of
affairs; but they also believed in the mystic
truth that "hatred ceaseth not by hatred
but by love"; and it was incumbent upon
the Muslims not to retaliate in anger. They
must have patience and try to win the
heart of their fellow-countrymen with a
positive approach of love and friendship. . . .

Above all, Deoband was convinced that
the western-educated League leadership
was exploiting the fair name of Islam for
the worldly gain of the Muslim vested interests which, knowing fully well that the
ignorant Muslim masses could only be won
over by appealing to their religious emotions, had given the slogan that in a united
India Islam would be in danger. As indicated before, the Deoband conception of
Islam was mainly in a legal form. It was
traditional, orthodox and conservative. It
could not accept any new interpretation of
Islam. But it is also significant that the
League leadership, mainly cut off from the
Islamic past and educated in a different
mould of intellectual traditions, failed to
produce an Islamic ideology. There was
nothing positive in its programme. The
Muslim League remained a negative move-

ment through and through. Its responsible
leaders always evaded all the basic questions put forward by their followers as well
as opponents. Even Aligarh, which can le-
gitimately be called the intellectual arsenal
of the movement, remained, till the last
moment, confused about the kind of society
that was going to be built up in Pakistan.
Islamic democracy, Islamic socialism and
terms like these were frequently used,
but what they meant by them was never
elaborated. For this intellectual bankruptcy
and ideological confusion Pakistan had subsequently to pay a very high price, in spite
of the sincere efforts of some of its leaders
to improve the situation.

Deoband was, however, certain that men
like Mr. Jinnāḥ and Nawābzādah Liyāqat
'Alī Khān were incapable of building up
an Islamic state in Pakistan. Neither their
educational training nor their mental make-
up was suited to strive for such a high
ideal. Experiences had shown that they had
no respect for the tenets of the "Sharī'ah."
They spoke of the comprehensiveness of
the Islamic law when they had to address
the Muslims in order to win their support
for their leadership; but in legislatures and
in private life they did not care for its application. . . .

Although there were leaders who, from
the League platform, gave the impression
that in Pakistan a sort of Islamic state based
on the principles of the Qur'ān and the
Sunnah, would be established, yet Mr.
Jinnāḥ himself seemed very clear about the
problem in so far as the nature of the
future constitution of Pakistan was concerned. It is true that there are some casual
references in his various statements and
speeches to Islam, the Qur'ān and the traditions of the Prophet; but it is also true
that he never dreamt of making Pakistan
a religious state. He was certainly inspired
by the Kamalist Revolution and, perhaps,
aspired to make the same experiment in
Pakistan as Mustafā Kamāl had done in
Turkey. In 1938 he exhorted the Muslims
at Patna to be up and doing by remarking
that in Kamāl Ataturk the Islamic world

had lost a great hero. With the example of that great man in front of them as an inspiration, would the Muslims of India remain in quagmire? In March, 1948, replying to the speech made by the first Turkish ambassador to Pakistan, he said "the exploits of your leaders in many a historic field of battle, the progress of your Revolution, the rise and career of the great Ataturk, his revitalisation of your nation by his great statesmanship, courage and foresight — all these stirring events are well-known to the people of Pakistan." On 11 August, 1947, delivering his presidential address to the Constituent Assembly of Pakistan, he declared:

You may belong to any religion or caste or creed — that has nothing to do with the business of the State. . . . You will find that in course of time Hindus would cease to be Hindus and Muslims would cease to be Muslims, not in the religious sense, because that is the personal faith of each individual, but in the political sense as citizens of the State.

These remarks of Mr. Jinnāḥ have been quoted to give a glimpse of his ideas and intentions regarding the nature of the Pakistani State and Government. The 'ulamā' were aware of this and this is why, conservative and orthodox as they were, they were unwilling to support a scheme which they interpreted as being sheerly worldly and which meant, according to them, a very high price in terms of the future plight of Islam and the Muslims in divided India.

III. THE FINAL RUPTURE

The Gandhi-Jinnah Correspondence

SIR FREDERICK PUCKLE

During World War II one of the Congress leaders, Chakravarti Rajago-
palochri, was not content to stand by and witness the widening gulf between
the party of Gandhi and that of Jinnah. In 1942 he advocated the acceptance
of the League's claim to a separate Muslim state, but he did not convince his
colleagues. He persisted in his efforts for a Congress-League conciliation, and
in the summer of 1944 wrote to Jinnah proposing a formula for an agreement.
This proposal was not accepted by the League leader but Jinnah did agree to
discuss the matter with Gandhi. The following account of the conversations was
written by Sir Frederick Puckle, the Director-General, Central Board of Information, Government of India.

THE two men met at Mr. Jinnah's
house in Bombay, while India waited
with mixed feelings for the result. Hindus,
for whom India means Hindustan, were
frankly apprehensive. They were vehe-
mently opposed to any splitting up of India
and some enthusiasts even picketed Mr.
Gandhi's lodgings as a protest against the
meeting. Congressmen, to whatever community they belonged, were nervous lest
Mr. Gandhi should prejudice the cause of
Indian independence and the Party's own
position by going too far in meeting Mr.
Jinnah's demands. The Moslem League
watched, confident in their President's ability to hold his own. Opinion generally was
pessimistic about the chances that the conversations would achieve much. The pes-
simists were right. On September 26, after
discussions lasting nearly three weeks, Mr.
Gandhi and Mr. Jinnah announced that
they had been unable to reach any agreement; the discussions were postponed *sine
die*, but not, they hoped, finally. The two
men parted with protestations of friendship, but it seems with some underlying
feeling of bitterness. They have since been
busy in explaining to their followers their
respective positions in terms studiously po-
lite but not always very conciliatory.

It appears that at the first meeting on
September 9, after some preliminary exposition of their views by both, Mr. Gandhi
invited Mr. Jinnah to "formulate in writing" the points which he thought required
explanation and clarification. Out of this
grew a voluminous correspondence, to
which the two men began to attach more
and more importance as a record of the
conversations. This correspondence, consisting of 21 letters, has been released.

In the last letter (September 26) Mr.

From Sir Frederick Puckle, "The Gandhi-Jinnah Conversations," *Foreign Affairs* (January 1945),
pp. 319–322, 323. Reprinted by permission of *Foreign Affairs*. Articles in *Foreign Affairs* are copy-
righted by the Council on Foreign Relations, Inc., New York.

Jinnah writes, "If a break comes, it will be because you have not satisfied me in regard to the essence of the Lahore Resolution." This was a resolution of the full session of the Moslem League at Lahore in March 1940, at which 100,000 Moslems were estimated to have been present. The essence of it was the "two nation" theory and everything which flows from its adoption. The resolution set forth the meaning of Pakistan, though the word Pakistan was not to be found in it. Once Mr. Gandhi and Mr. Jinnah disagreed about the two nation theory, they disagreed inevitably on Pakistan and on every other point which came up in their discussion.

Mr. Jinnah expounded the Moslem position in the following words:

We maintain that Moslems and Hindus are two major nations by any definition or test of a nation. We are a nation of a hundred million, and what is more we are a nation with our distinctive culture and civilization, language and literature, art and architecture, names and nomenclature, sense of value and proportion, legal laws and moral codes, customs and calendar, history and traditions, aptitudes and ambitions. In short, we have our distinctive outlook on life and of life. By all canons of international law, we are a nation.

To this Mr. Gandhi replied:

I can find no parallel in history for a body of converts and their descendants claiming to be a nation apart from the parent stock. If India was one nation before the advent of Islam, it must remain one in spite of a change of the faith of a very large body of her children. You do not claim to be a separate nation by right of conquest but by reason of the acceptance of Islam. Will the two nations become one if the whole of India accepted Islam? Will Bengalis, Oriyas, Andhras, Tamilians, Maharashtrians, Gujaratis, cease to have their special characteristics if all of them become converts to Islam?

For practical purposes, there was no more discussion. Mr. Gandhi remarked that the mere assertion that Hindus and Moslems

were two nations was no proof. No more, of course, was an assertion to the contrary. So while he continued to declare that he saw nothing but ruin for the whole of India, if the theory were accepted, and Mr. Jinnah continued to maintain that the true welfare not only of Moslems but of the rest of India lay in such a division of India, and that this was the road to the achievement of freedom and independence for all, the matter was really taken no further. It is, of course, a proposition which is hardly susceptible of proof; creeds rarely are.

Once we grasp the importance which the two nation theory has for Mr. Jinnah, and the finality of Mr. Gandhi's rejection of it, the rest of the discussion, as revealed in the letters, becomes comprehensible. A number of points were taken up, most of which arose out of Mr. Rajagopalachari's original formula, or an alternative to it which Mr. Gandhi propounded in his letter of September 24. Mr. Jinnah commented that the two formulas had a family resemblance and in essence were much the same. It will be sufficient to examine the fundamentals of Mr. Gandhi's own formula and Mr. Jinnah's objections to them.

What we may call the preamble laid down two assumptions: (1) That India is not to be regarded as two or more nations but as one family consisting of many members. (2) That the Moslem members of the family living in Baluchistan, Sind, North West Frontier Province and that part of the Punjab where they are in an absolute majority and in those parts of Bengal and Assam where they are in an absolute majority, desire to live in separation from the rest of India.

On these assumptions, Mr. Gandhi proposed: (1) That the claim to separation should be accepted. (2) That the areas eligible for separation should be demarcated by a joint Congress-League Commission. (3) That there should be a plebiscite of all the inhabitants of these areas. (4) That where the vote was in favor of separation, separate states should be formed "as soon as possible after India is free from foreign domination and can therefore be constituted into two sovereign independent states." (5) That there should be a treaty of separation providing for the administration "of foreign affairs, defense, internal communications, commerce and the like, which must necessarily continue to be matters of common interest between the contracting parties." (6) That the Congress and the League should, "Immediately on the acceptance of this agreement" (i.e., Mr. Gandhi's formula, not the treaty in clause 5) decide upon a course of common action for the attainment of independence for India, but that the League would not be bound to join the Congress in any "direct action."

How with this preamble, which directly denied the fundamental principle of the Lahore Resolution — the two nation theory — Mr. Gandhi hoped to obtain acceptance of the rest of his proposal is not clear. Mr. Jinnah's letter of September 25 is a detailed rejection of it, which for practical purposes closed the conversations, though there were two or three subsequent letters. Mr. Jinnah was consistent. Since the Moslems were a separate nation, the right of self-determination rested in them and them alone. . . . "Ours," he wrote, "is a case of carving out two independent sovereign states by way of settlement between major nations, Hindus and Moslems, and not of severance or secession from any existing union." . . . Mr. Jinnah refused a general plebiscite and maintained his position that where Moslems were in a majority . . . , it was for Moslems, and Moslems alone, to decide whether they wished to separate from the rest of India. If they did so decide . . . subsequent territorial adjustments, to avoid including in Pakistan predominantly Hindu districts, were not ruled out.

Mr. Jinnah also rejected clause five, which laid down that a treaty should be concluded to "provide for the efficient and satisfactory administration" of foreign affairs and other "matters of common interest." . . . On September 21 Mr. Jinnah

had replied that there could be no "defense and similar matters of common concern"; this was a question to be settled by the constitution-making body chosen by Pakistan, negotiating with a similar body from Hindustan and both representing sovereign states.

In the letter of September 25, he implies that Mr. Gandhi had some central machinery in mind (perhaps this had been suggested verbally) and goes on to affirm that "these matters, which are the lifeblood of any state, cannot be delegated to any central authority or government; they will have to be dealt with on the assumption that Pakistan and Hindustan are two independent states." . . .

The remaining clauses of Mr. Gandhi's offer may be summed up, in effect, as a suggestion that . . . Hindus and Moslems should combine to force the British to declare India independent and hand over authority to a provisional national government. At their leisure they could then frame the new constitution and settle the details of the division between Hindustan and Pakistan. . . . One can understand that Mr. Jinnah was logically bound to reject the preliminary agreement in the form in which it was put to him. . . .

Why is Mr. Jinnah so suspicious of the Congress Party that he will not join with it to gain that independence . . . until he has got in his pocket security for the Moslems, which is what Pakistan means? That this mistrust exists comes out very clearly in his letter of September 23. . . . he asserts that the Congress planned a constituent assembly [after independence but before any agreement on partition] "composed of an overwhelming majority of Hindus, nearly 75 per cent"; he talks of these demands being made enforceable "at your [Gandhi's] command and when ordered by you as sole dictator of the Congress Party. . . ."

Looked at from this distant range, there seem to have been two main reasons why no definite results came out of the discussions. The first was that Mr. Jinnah demanded the acceptance in full of the two nation doctrine and Mr. Gandhi knew he could not carry his followers with him in accepting this demand. The second was that the weaker party, the Moslems, is deeply suspicious of the stronger party, the Hindus, and Mr. Jinnah will not give up his strongest lever, Moslem aid in bringing pressure on the British Government to accelerate transfer of power to a national Indian Government, until he has the price in his hands — Moslem security, or Pakistan.

The Mission Plan Was Practicable

MAULANA AZAD

One of the most distinguished Indian nationalists was the Muslim scholar Maulana Azad. A colleague of Gandhi, he participated in several noncooperation movements, and was imprisoned by the British on a number of occasions. Unlike Jinnah, Maulana Azad remained in the National Congress and during the difficult years of World War II served as its president. He believed that the Congress was a truly national and secular body comprehensive enough to include both Muslims and Hindus, and any other religious groups, within its ranks. The following selection is taken from Maulana Azad's autobiography, written when he was serving as education minister in Nehru's government. These personal reflections are extremely valuable. When the book was published in 1959, it created somewhat of a sensation both for its belief that the Cabinet Mission's plan was practicable and also for the criticism leveled at Nehru for its failure. Another noted Indian educator, Humayun Kabir, assisted in the preparation of the volume and in the preface reveals that some thirty pages of the text were deleted and placed in the National Archives. This material, when available, will likely throw more light on partition.

I WAS listening to the radio at 9:30 in the evening on 17 February 1946 when I heard the report of the new British decision. Lord Pethick Lawrence had announced in Parliament that the British Government would send a Cabinet Mission to India to discuss with the representatives of India the question of Indian freedom. This was also outlined in the Viceroy's speech on the same date. The Mission was to consist of Lord Pethick Lawrence, Secretary of State for India, Sir Stafford Cripps, the President of the Board of Trade, and Mr. A. V. Alexander, the First Lord of the Admiralty. Within half an hour, a representative of the Associated Press arrived and asked me about my reactions.

I told him that I was glad the Labour Government had taken a decisive step. I was also pleased that the Mission which was coming included Sir Stafford Cripps, who had already carried on negotiations with us and was therefore an old friend. . . .

The Cabinet Mission arrived in India on 23 March. Mr. J. C. Gupta, a prominent Congressman of Bengal, had acted as host to Sir Stafford Cripps when he came to India on an earlier occasion. He told me he was going to Delhi to meet Cripps. I gave him a letter for Sir Stafford welcoming him back to India.

I reached Delhi on 2 April 1946. It seemed to me that the most important subject for consideration at this stage was not the political issue between India and Britain but the communal question in India. The Simla Conference had convinced me that the political question had reached a stage of settlement. The communal differences were still unresolved.

From Maulana Abul Kalam Azad, *India Wins Freedom* (Bombay: Orient Longmans), pp. 138–191. Reprinted by permission of Orient Longmans Ltd.

One thing nobody could deny. As a community, the Muslims were extremely anxious about their future. It is true that they were in a clear majority in certain provinces. At the provincial level they had therefore no fears in these areas. They were however a minority in India as a whole and were troubled by the fear that their position and status in independent India would not be secure.

I gave continuous and anxious thought to this subject. All over the world, the tendency was for the decentralization of power. In a country so vast as India and with people so diverse in language, customs and geographical conditions, a unitary government was obviously most unsuitable. Decentralization of power in a federal government would also help to allay the fears of the minorities. Ultimately I came to the conclusion that the Constitution of India must, from the nature of the case, be federal. Further, it must be so framed as to ensure autonomy to the provinces in as many subjects as possible. We had to reconcile the claims of provincial autonomy and national unity. This could be done by finding a satisfactory formula for the distribution of powers and functions between the Central and the provincial governments. Some powers and functions would be essentially central, others essentially provincial and some which could be either, would be provincially or centrally exercised by consent. The first step was to devise a formula by which a minimum number of subjects should be declared as essentially the responsibility of the Central Government. These must belong to the Union Government compulsorily. In addition, there should be a list of subjects which could be dealt with centrally if the provinces so desired. This might be called the optional list for the Central Government and any province which so wished could delegate its powers in respect of all or any of these subjects to the Central Government.

It was clear to me that Defence, Communications and Foreign Affairs were subjects which could be dealt with adequately only on an all-India basis. Any attempt to deal with them on a provincial level would defeat the purpose and destroy the very basis of a federal Government. Certain other subjects would be equally obviously a provincial responsibility, but there should be a third list of subjects where the provincial legislature would decide whether to retain them as provincial subjects or delegate them to the Centre.

The more I thought about the matter, the clearer it became to me that the Indian problem could not be solved on any other lines. If a constitution were to be framed which embodied this principle, it would ensure that in the Muslim majority provinces, all subjects except three could be administered by the province itself. This would eliminate from the minds of the Muslims all fears of domination by the Hindus. Once such fears were allayed, it was likely that the provinces would find it an advantage to delegate some other subjects as well to the Central Government. I was also satisfied that, even apart from communal considerations, this was the best political solution for a country like India. India is a vast country with a large population divided into more or less homogeneous units which live in different provinces. It was necessary to ensure to the provinces the largest possible measure of autonomy even on general considerations of constitutional propriety and practical administration.

This picture had gradually formed in my mind and had become quite clear by the time the Cabinet Mission came to India though I had not so far discussed it with my colleagues. I thought that I should state my position in clear and unambiguous terms when the proper time came.

I met the Members of the Cabinet Mission for the first time on 6 April 1946. The Mission had framed some questions for discussion. The first one dealt with the communal problem in India. When the Mission asked me how I would tackle the communal situation, I indicated the solution I had already framed. As soon as I said that the Centre should have a minimum list of compulsory subjects and an additional list of optional ones, Lord Pethick Lawrence said, "You are in fact suggesting a new solution of the communal problem." . . .

The Working Committee met on 12 April when I reported on my discussions with the Cabinet Mission. I described in somewhat greater detail the solution of the communal problem I had suggested. This was the first time that Gandhiji and my colleagues had an opportunity of discussing my scheme. The Working Committee was initially somewhat sceptical about the solution and members raised all kinds of difficulties and doubts. I was able to meet their objections and clarified doubtful points. Finally the Working Committee was convinced about the soundness of the proposal and Gandhiji expressed his complete agreement with the solution. . . .

The Muslim League had for the first time spoken of a possible division of India in its Lahore Resolution. This later came to be known as the Pakistan Resolution. The solution I suggested was intended to meet the fears of the Muslim League. Now that I had discussed my scheme with my colleagues and members of the Cabinet Mission, I felt that the time had come to place it before the country. Accordingly on 15 April 1946, I issued a statement dealing with the demands of Muslims and other minorities. Now that the division of India is a fact and ten years have passed, I again look at the statement and find that everything I had then said has come about. As this statement contains my considered views on the solution of the Indian problem, I feel I should quote it. This is what I said then and would still say:

I have considered from every possible point of view the scheme of Pakistan as formulated by the Muslim League. As an Indian, I have examined its implications for the future of India as a whole. As a Muslim I have examined its likely effects upon the fortunes of Muslims of India.

Considering the scheme in all its aspects I have come to the conclusion that it is harmful not only for India as a whole but for Muslims in particular. And in fact it creates more problems than it solves. . . .

Two states confronting one another offer no solution of the problem of one another's minorities, but only lead to retribution and reprisals by introducing a system of mutual hostages. The scheme of Pakistan therefore solves no problem for the Muslims. It cannot safeguard their rights where they are in a minority nor as citizens of Pakistan secure them a position in Indian or world affairs which they would enjoy as citizens of a major State like the Indian Union. . . .

The formula which I have succeeded in making the Congress accept secures whatever merit the Pakistan scheme contains while all its defects and drawbacks are avoided. The basis of Pakistan is fear of interference by the Centre in Muslim majority areas as the Hindus will be in a majority in the Centre. The Congress meets this fear by granting full autonomy to the provincial units and vesting all residuary power in the provinces. It has also provided for two lists of Central subjects, one compulsory and one optional, so that if any provincial unit so wants, it can administer all subjects except a minimum delegated to the Centre. The Congress scheme therefore ensures that Muslim majority provinces are internally free to develop as they will, but can at the same time influence the Centre on all issues which affect India as a whole. . . .

I have already mentioned that the Cabinet Mission published its scheme on 16 May. Basically, it was the same as the one sketched in my statement of 15 April. The Cabinet Mission Plan provided that only three subjects would belong compulsorily to the Central Government. . . . The Mission had also accepted my view that the majority of subjects would be treated at the provincial level. Muslims in the majority provinces would thus exercise almost complete autonomy. . . . Since the Cabinet Mission Plan was in spirit the same as mine and the only addition was the institution of the three Sections, I felt that we should accept the proposal. . . .

The Muslim League Council met for

three days before it could come to a decision. On the final day, Jinnah had to admit that there could be no fairer solution of the minority problem than that presented in the Cabinet Mission Plan. In any case he could not get better terms. He told the Council that the scheme presented by the Cabinet Mission was the maximum that he could secure. As such, he advised the Muslim League to accept the scheme and the Council voted unanimously in its favour. . . . After protracted negotiations, the Working Committee [of Congress] in its resolution of 26 June accepted the Cabinet Mission's Plan for the future, though it found itself unable to accept the proposal for an interim government. . . .

The acceptance of the Cabinet Mission Plan by both Congress and the Muslim League was a glorious event in the history of the freedom movement in India. It meant that the difficult question of Indian freedom had been settled by negotiation and agreement and not by methods of violence and conflict. It also seemed that the communal difficulties had been finally left behind. Throughout the country there was a deep sense of jubilation and all the people were united in their demand for freedom. We rejoiced but we did not then know that our joy was premature and bitter disappointment awaited us.

The Muslim League Council had accepted the Cabinet Mission Plan. So had the Congress Working Committee. It however needed the approval of the A.I.C.C. We thought this would be a formal matter as the A.I.C.C. had always ratified the decision of the Working Committee. . . .

The Working Committee met on 6 July and prepared draft resolutions for the consideration of the A.I.C.C. The first resolution dealt with the Cabinet Mission Plan. I was asked to move it, as strenuous opposition was expected from the leftist group in the Congress.

When the A.I.C.C. met, I invited Jawaharlal to take over as Congress President from me. . . . Then I moved the reso-

lution on the Cabinet Mission Plan and spoke briefly about its main features. . . . My speech had a decisive influence on the audience. When the vote was taken the resolution was passed with an overwhelming majority. Thus the seal of approval was put on the Working Committee's resolution accepting the Cabinet Mission Plan.

After a few days, I received telegrams of congratulation from Lord Pethick Lawrence and Sir Stafford Cripps. They were happy that the A.I.C.C. had accepted my resolution and congratulated me on my able presentation of the Cabinet Mission Plan.

Now happened one of those unfortunate events which changed the course of history. On 10 July Jawaharlal held a Press Conference in Bombay in which he made a statement which in normal circumstances might have passed almost unnoticed, but in the existing atmosphere of suspicion and hatred, set in train a most unfortunate series of consequences. Some Press representatives asked him whether with the passing of the Resolution by the A.I.C.C., the Congress had accepted the plan *in toto,* including the composition of the Interim Government.

Jawaharlal stated in reply that Congress would enter the Constituent Assembly "completely unfettered by agreements and free to meet all situations as they arise."

Press representatives further asked if this meant that the Cabinet Mission Plan could be modified.

Jawaharlal replied emphatically that the Congress had agreed only to participate in the Constituent Assembly and regarded itself free to change or modify the Cabinet Mission Plan as it thought best.

I must place on record that Jawaharlal's statement was wrong. It was not correct to say that Congress was free to modify the Plan as it pleased. We had in fact agreed that the Central Government would be federal. There would be the compulsory list of three Central subjects while all other subjects remained in the provincial sphere. We had further agreed that there would be the three Sections, viz., A, B, and C, in which the provinces would be grouped. These matters could not be changed unilaterally by Congress without the consent of other parties to the agreement.

The Muslim League had accepted the Cabinet Mission Plan, as this represented the utmost limit to which the British Government would go. In his speech to the League Council, Mr. Jinnah had clearly stated that he recommended acceptance only because nothing better could be obtained.

Mr. Jinnah was thus not very happy about the outcome of the negotiations . . . Jawaharlal's statement came to him as a bombshell. He immediately issued a statement that this declaration by the Congress President demanded a review of the whole situation. . . . Now that the Congress President had declared that the Congress could change the scheme through its majority in the Constituent Assembly, this would mean that the minorities were placed at the mercy of the majority. His view was that Jawaharlal's declaration meant that Congress had rejected the Cabinet Mission Plan and as such the Viceroy should call upon the Muslim League, which had accepted the Plan, to form a government.

The Muslim League Council met at Bombay on 27 July. In his opening speech Mr. Jinnah reiterated the demand for Pakistan as the only course left open for the Muslim League. After three days' discussion, the Council passed a resolution rejecting the Cabinet Mission Plan. It also decided to resort to direct action for the achievement of Pakistan.

The 16th of August was a black day in the history of India. Unprecedented mob violence plunged the great city of Calcutta into an orgy of bloodshed, murder and terror. Hundreds of lives were lost. Thousands were injured and property worth crores of rupees was destroyed. Processions were taken out by the League which began to loot and commit acts of arson. Soon the whole city was in the grip of goondaas [hooligans and thugs]. . . .

The 16th of August 1946 was a black day not only for Calcutta but for the whole of India. The turn that events had taken made it almost impossible to expect a peaceful solution by agreement between the Congress and the Muslim League. This was one of the greatest tragedies of Indian history and I have to say with the deepest regret that it had followed inexorably from the opportunity given to the Muslim League to reopen the whole question of political and communal settlement. Mr. Jinnah took full advantage of this mistake and withdrew from the League's early acceptance of the Cabinet Mission Plan.

Jawaharlal is one of my dearest friends and his contribution to India's national life is second to none. He has worked and suffered for Indian freedom, and since the attainment of independence, he has become the symbol of our national unity and progress. I have nevertheless to say with regret that he is at times apt to be carried away by his feelings. Not only so, but sometimes he is so impressed by theoretical considerations that he is apt to underestimate the realities of a situation.

His fondness for abstract theory was responsible for his statement about the Constituent Assembly. . . .

Lord Mountbatten first became well known during the war years. . . . When the war ended, he returned to Britain, but on Lord Wavell's resignation he was appointed Viceroy and Governor-General. Fully briefed by the Labour Government before he left, he came with instructions from Mr. Attlee that power must be transferred before June 1948.

He reached Delhi on 22 March and was sworn in as Viceroy and Governor-General of India on the 24th. Immediately after the swearing-in ceremony, he made a short speech, in which he stressed the need for reaching a solution within the next few months.

Soon after this, I had my first interview with Lord Mountbatten. At the very first meeting he told me that the British Government was fully determined to transfer power. Before this could happen, a settlement of the communal problem was necessary and he desired that a final and decisive attempt must be made to solve the problem. . . .

In the meantime, the situation was deteriorating every day. The Calcutta riots had been followed by risings in Noakhali and Bihar. Thereafter there was trouble in Bombay. The Punjab, which had been quiet till now, also showed signs of strain and conflict. . . .

The situation was made worse by the deadlock between the Congress and the Muslim League within the Executive Council. The Central Government was paralyzed by the way in which the Members of the Council pulled against one another. The League was in charge of Finance and held the key to the administration. . . .

A truly pathetic situation had developed as a result of the Congress mistake in giving Finance to the Muslim League. This had led to the deadlock which gave Lord Mountbatten the opportunity of slowly preparing the ground for the partition of India. As he began to give a new turn to the political problem he tried to impress on Congress the inevitability of partition, and sowed the seeds of the idea in the minds of the Congress Members of the Executive Council.

It must be placed on record that the man in India who first fell for Lord Mountbatten's idea was Sardar Patel. . . . The situation within the Executive Council had so annoyed and irritated Sardar Patel that he now became a believer in partition. . . . When Lord Mountbatten suggested that partition might offer a solution for the present difficulty, he found ready acceptance of the idea in Sardar Patel's mind. He was convinced that he could not work with the Muslim League. He openly said that he was prepared to let the League have a part of India if only he could get rid of it. . . .

As soon as Sardar Patel had been convinced, Lord Mountbatten turned his attention to Jawaharlal. Jawaharlal was not at first willing and reacted violently against the very idea of partition, but Lord Mountbatten persisted till step by step Jawahar-

lal's opposition was worn down. Within a month of Lord Mountbatten's arrival in India Jawaharlal, the firm opponent of partition, had become, if not a supporter, at least acquiescent towards the idea. . . .

When I became aware that Lord Mountbatten was thinking in terms of dividing India and had persuaded Jawaharlal and Patel, I was deeply distressed. I realized that the country was moving towards a great danger. The partition of India would be harmful not only to Muslims but to the whole country. I was and am still convinced that the Cabinet Mission Plan was the best solution. . . .

I did my best to persuade my two colleagues not to take the final step. I found that Patel was so much in favour of partition that he was hardly prepared even to listen to any other point of view. . . .

I was surprised and pained when Patel . . . said that whether we liked it or not, there were two nations in India. He was now convinced that Muslims and Hindus could not be united into one nation. There was no alternative except to recognize this fact. . . .

Jawaharlal spoke to me in sorrow but left no doubt in my mind as to how his mind was working. It was clear that in spite of his repugnance to the idea of partition, he was coming to the conclusion day by day that there was no alternative. He recognized that partition was evil, but he held that circumstances were inevitably leading in that direction. . . .

Gandhiji remained my only hope. . . . I went to see him at once and his very first remark was,

Partition has now become a threat. It seems Vallabhbhai Patel and even Jawaharlal have surrendered. If the Congress wishes to accept partition, it will be over my dead body. So long as I am alive, I will never agree to the partition of India. Nor will I, if I can help it, allow Congress to accept it.

Later that day Gandhiji met Lord Mountbatten. He saw him again the next day and still again on 2 April. Sardar Patel came to him soon after he returned from his first meeting with Lord Mountbatten and was closeted with him for over two hours. What happened during this meeting I do not know. But when I met Gandhiji again, I received the greatest shock of my life, for I found that he too had changed. . . .

I thought deeply over the whole matter. How was it that Gandhiji could change his opinion so quickly? My reading is that this was due to the influence of Sardar Patel. Patel openly said that there was no way out except partition. Experience has shown that it was impossible to work with the Muslim League. Another consideration probably weighed with Sardar Patel. Lord Mountbatten had argued that Congress had agreed to a weak Centre only in order to meet the objection of the League. Provinces were therefore given full provincial autonomy, but in a country so divided by language, community and culture, a weak Centre was bound to encourage fissiparous tendencies. If the Muslim League were not there, we could plan for a strong Central Government and frame a constitution desirable from the point of view of Indian unity. Lord Mountbatten advised that it would be better to give up a few small pieces in the north-west and the north-east and then build up a strong and consolidated India. . . . It seemed to me that these arguments had influenced not only Sardar Patel but Jawaharlal. The same arguments repeated by Sardar Patel and Lord Mountbatten had also weakened Gandhiji's opposition to partition.

My effort throughout had been to persuade Lord Mountbatten to take a firm stand on the Cabinet Mission Plan. So long as Gandhiji was of the same view, I had not lost hope. Now with the change in Gandhiji's view, I knew that Lord Mountbatten would not agree to my suggestion. It is also possible that Lord Mountbatten did not feel so strongly about the Cabinet Mission Plan, as this was not the child of his brain. It is therefore not surprising that as soon as he met with strong opposition to the Cabinet Mission Plan, he was willing to substitute for it a plan of partition formulated according to his own ideas. . . .

By this time Lord Mountbatten had framed his own proposals for the partition of India. He now decided to go to London for discussions with the British Government and to secure their approval to his proposals. . . .

I had a lingering hope that the Labour Cabinet would not easily accept the rejection of the Cabinet Mission Plan. It was framed by three members of the Cabinet who were also important members of the Labour movement. . . . It was therefore with regret that I heard soon after Lord Mountbatten reached London that the British Cabinet had accepted the scheme proposed by him.

The details of Lord Mountbatten's Plan were not yet published but I guessed that it would entail the partition of India. He returned to Delhi on 30 May and on 2 June held discussions with the representatives of the Congress and the Muslim League. On the 3rd of June a White Paper was issued which gave all the details of the Plan. The price for freedom was the partitioning of India into two States.

The Cabinet Mission: Nehru's Role

MICHAEL BRECHER

Michael Brecher, Professor of Political Science at McGill University, is the author of what is generally considered the best biography of Jawaharlal Nehru. In the following selection, after summarizing the plan of the Cabinet Mission that was presented to the Indian parties in 1946, he analyzes Nehru's attitude to it. This interpretation should be contrasted with that of Maulana Azad in the preceding statement.

THE initial announcement about the Cabinet Mission was obscure on the approach to a settlement. Attlee filled in the gaps in a statement before the House of Commons on 15 March 1946. It was the turn of the Congress to be reassured. On the core issue of independence the British Prime Minister declared:

India herself must choose what will be her future Constitution. I hope that the Indian people may elect to remain within the British Commonwealth. . . . But if she does so elect, it must be by her own free will. . . . If, on the other hand, she elects for independence, in our view she has a right to do so.

As for the Muslim League's goal of Pakistan, he said:

We are very mindful of the rights of minorities and minorities should be able to live free from fear. On the other hand, we cannot allow a minority to place a veto on the advance of the majority.

The Congress was jubilant, the League dismayed by this unexpected shift of policy. Both marshalled their forces for a showdown.

Cripps was the dominant figure in the Cabinet Mission, the person who produced the complex plans which attempted to please every shade of political opinion but satisfied no one. The Mission's goals were twofold — to reconstitute the Viceroy's Executive Council as a coalition Interim Government and to secure agreement on a constitution-making body. The "three wise men" arived in Delhi on 24 March and began a round of interviews with representatives of all political parties. After a brief adjournment to Kashmir, Pethick Lawrence, the senior member of the Mission, conveyed the bases of a compromise settlement to the Congress and League Presidents.

The "fundamental principles" of the scheme were deceptively simple. There was to be

a Union Government dealing with . . . Foreign Affairs, Defence and Communications . . . [and] two groups of Provinces, the one of the predominantly Hindu Provinces and the other of the predominantly Muslim Provinces, dealing with all other subjects which the Provinces in the respective groups desire to be dealt with in common. The Provincial Governments will deal with all other subjects

From Michael Brecher, *Nehru, A Political Biography* (London, 1959), pp. 309–311, 315–318. Reprinted by permission of Oxford University Press.

73

and will have all the residuary Sovereign rights. It is contemplated that the Indian [princely] States will take their appropriate place in this structure on terms to be negotiated with them.

This three-tier plan was drafted by Cripps at breakfast one morning in Delhi just after his return from Kashmir.

For the next few months a battle of interpretation raged fiercely in the Indian capital, reflecting the complexity of the scheme, the intensity of feelings and the depth of disagreement between the Congress and the League. The Mission itself was to add to the confusion by its successive "clarifications."

The negotiations began with a cautious, qualified acceptance by both parties of the invitations to discuss these "fundamental principles" at Simla. From the outset the lines of division were clearly drawn by the Congress and the League. Their spokesmen moved to Simla early in May, with Nehru, Azad, Patel and Abdul Ghaffar Khan acting for the Congress, Jinnah, Liaquat Ali, Mishtar and Mohammed Ismail representing the League. Gandhi attended at the Mission's request because Cripps was determined to avoid a repetition of the 1942 fiasco. Minor concessions were made in an effort to secure agreement, but to no avail. On fundamental issues the impasse was complete. The Congress insisted that the Union Constitution be framed first, the League, after the Group Constitutions were drafted. The Congress insisted on the optional character of the Groups, the League demanded that they be compulsory. The Congress insisted on the right of the Union to raise revenue by taxation, the League refused. After a week of fruitless negotiations the second Simla Conference came to an end.

The Cabinet Mission now offered its own recommendations in two instalments: on 16 May it announced a long-range plan, i.e., proposals for a constitutional settlement; and on 16 June it outlined a procedure for the formation of an Interim Government. . . . There were to be three Sections for British India: B, consisting of the Muslim-majority provinces in the northwest, namely, the Punjab, Sind, the North-West Frontier Province and Baluchistan; C, consisting of Bengal and Assam; and A, the rest of British India. The Sections would meet to form Groups and to draft the provincial and group constitutions. Each province would have the right to opt out of a Group by a simple majority of its legislature after the first elections under the new provincial constitutions. Thus the League was offered a *de facto* Pakistan. The Congress could find in the scheme a united India, though somewhat emasculated, and an assurance of provincial autonomy. The plan also provided for the lapse of Paramountcy, thereby granting freedom of action to the Princes. . . .

The League accepted the plan "inasmuch as the basis and the foundation of Pakistan are inherent in the Mission's plan by virtue of compulsory grouping of the six Muslim Provinces . . ." — which included the Hindu-majority province of Assam. The Congress played for time. . . .

The next stage in the tangled story of the Cabinet Mission began early in July 1946, when the A.I.C.C. met in Bombay to consider the Mission's plans. The debate was spirited, but the outcome was never in doubt. The policy enunciated by the Working Committee was approved by 204 to 51. Yet the Congress was unhappy about the plans, as evident in Nehru's speech on 10 July, one of the most fiery and provocative statements in his forty years of public life.

The Congress was committed to participate in the Constituent Assembly, he said, but nothing else. And the Assembly would be a sovereign body, regardless of policy statements from London. Of course, protection of the minorities had to be assured, as Congress had always pledged, but this would be done by the Constituent Assembly alone. As for a treaty with Britain, this would depend on British attitude. If they tried to delay the transfer of power, he said, there would be a direct clash. If they treated Indians as equals there would be a treaty, but any attempt to impose it would be resisted. About the grouping scheme Nehru was brutally candid. It would probably never come to fruition, he declared, because section A, the Hindu-majority provinces, would be opposed, the Frontier Province would oppose it in section B as would Assam in section C, and provincial jealousies would thwart it. He also stressed the likelihood of a much stronger central government than that envisaged by the Cabinet Mission. While its jurisdiction would be confined to foreign affairs, defence and communications, he said, each of these would be broadly interpreted and would probably include defence industries, foreign trade policy, loans, and taxing power for the Centre, "because it couldn't live on doles. . . . The scope of the Centre, even though limited, inevitably grows, because it cannot exist otherwise."

There was much political insight in Nehru's speech. Few would deny that the Frontier and Assam, both Congress provinces at the time, would opt out of their Groups if given an opportunity to do so in 1946. His reference to provincial jealousies found ample support in the post-partition history of West Pakistan and India. So too did his observations on a strong Centre; both India and Pakistan have had frequent recourse to emergency powers since Independence.

Whether it was wise to utter such views in the political atmosphere of 1946 is another question. Nehru's remarks certainly cleared the air of confusion and hypocrisy. At the same time they destroyed the facade of agreement which the Cabinet Mission tried to maintain. In fact, his speech sparked the collapse of the Mission. There was nothing fundamentally new in his speech, but it was a serious tactical error: Jinnah was given an incomparable wedge to press more openly for Pakistan on the grounds of Congress "tyranny." This was done on 27 July when the League withdrew its acceptance of the Mission's long-run plan and called for "Direct Action" to achieve the goal of Pakistan. The "Direct Action" decision was ominous, for it set in motion the disastrous civil war which was to engulf the sub-continent for the next eighteen months. August 16 was proclaimed "Direct Action Day." To the Council of the League Jinnah announced: "Today we bid goodbye to constitutional methods." The die was cast. The death knell to the Cabinet Mission's long-run plan had been sounded, though it was to linger on for another seven months.

Many persons regret that this plan never came to fruition. But it satisfied neither party and was unworkable in the tension of 1946–7. Neither the Congress nor the League ever really accepted the plan, though both placed their formal approval on record for bargaining purposes. It suffered from other disabilities as well. The Labour Government and its three envoys were sincere in wanting to transfer power, but none seemed to know how to accomplish it. By contrast, the India Office and some permanent officials in India opposed the transfer, especially as long as the Congress was committed to secession from the Commonwealth, as it then was.

The basic drawback of the plan was its complexity and cumbersome procedure. Cripps approached the highly-charged problem of a constitutional settlement as if it were an intellectual exercise. The three-tier scheme (Centre, Groups, provinces) was an intellectual *tour de force* but it was impracticable in the environment of a deadly struggle for power. It would have led to endless friction between the Centre, the Groups and the provinces, and between the Congress and the League, making normal administration impossible. Cripps apparently never thought out the consequences. He was riding two horses at the same time, trying to find a solution on paper which both parties would accept. His proposal in effect would have brought Pakistan in through the back door, by the group scheme, and would have maintained the facade of a united India. As long as the two Indian parties disagreed on fundamentals any plan was doomed, until the communal riots weakened the Congress will to persist in the demand for a united India. Such a disaster had yet to run its course.

The Cabinet Mission: Doomed from the Outset

PENDEREL MOON

Penderel Moon, a member of the Indian Civil Service at the time of Partition, was very close to the events he describes. He believes that the Cabinet Mission's plan, aimed at preventing the division of the country, was doomed from the outset because it did not take into account the basic differences between the Indian National Congress and the Muslim League over the future constitutional setup.

THE Cabinet Mission's arrival in Delhi coincided with the onset of the hot weather and the temperature steadily rose as they went through a round of preliminary interviews with representatives of the main political parties, the Indian States, the Sikhs, the scheduled castes, and not least, with Gandhi. . . .

Towards the end of April, after completing their round of interviews, the Mission took a short recess, expressing the hope that the main parties would themselves now come together and offer some agreed basis for framing the constitution. There was not the slightest prospect of any such thing occurring. Everyone knew that the Cabinet Mission would themselves have to propound their own scheme, and therein lay the only hope for finding a compromise. Several schemes had in fact been mooted during the course of the preliminary interviews and conversations. One of these, though not intrinsically the best, when adumbrated by Sir Stafford to Jinnah informally, seemed to awaken in that cold serpent-like figure a spark of interest, the scintilla of a positive response. Seeing the chance, Sir Stafford took it. The fundamental principles of this particular scheme were set down in writing and communicated on April 27th to both Congress and the League as a possible basis of agreement. Each was invited to send four negotiators to discuss them in the more temperate climate of Simla. These fundamental principles were as follows:

(i) A Union Government to deal only with foreign affairs, defence and communications;

(ii) two Groups of Provinces, one of the predominantly Hindu provinces, and the other of the predominantly Muslim provinces, to deal with such of the remaining subjects as the provinces in the respective groups desired to be dealt with in common;

(iii) the Provincial Governments to deal with all other subjects and to have all the residuary sovereign rights;

(iv) the Indian States to take their appropriate place in this structure on terms to be negotiated with them.

Both sides accepted the invitation, but both made it clear that this did not imply agreement with the fundamental principles. Jinnah merely reiterated his demand for a "six province" Pakistan and, as a corollary, the setting up of two separate

From Penderel Moon, *Divide and Quit* (London, 1961), pp. 45–64. Reprinted by permission of Chatto & Windus Ltd. and the University of California Press.

constitution-making bodies. Congress specified straight away their main objection to the proposed scheme. "We consider it wrong," they wrote, "to form Groups of Provinces under the Federal Union and more so on religious or communal basis. Any sub-federation within the Federal Union would weaken the Federal Centre and would otherwise be wrong. . . . It would result in creating three layers of executive and legislative bodies, an arrangement which will be cumbrous, static and disjointed, leading to continuous friction."

It will be seen that they objected to just those features of the scheme which carried the faint impression of Pakistan. They stuck to this objection to the bitter end.

The discussions in Simla, though comparatively cordial, led to no agreement, and it was left, therefore, to the Cabinet Mission and the Viceroy to rehash and elaborate the scheme in the light of the views expressed and to put it forward publicly as offering the best arrangement for providing a new constitution for an independent India. This they did in a carefully drafted statement issued on May 16th.

In this statement the proposal for "a separate and fully independent sovereign State of Pakistan as claimed by the Muslim League" was considered and decisively rejected. It was pointed out that a Pakistan of six provinces, as demanded by the League, would not solve the problem of communal minorities since twenty million Muslims would still remain in India and there would be non-Muslim minorities in Pakistan amounting to 38 per cent of the population in the western part and 48 per cent in the eastern part. "Nor can we see any justification," the statement went on, "for including within a sovereign Pakistan those districts of the Punjab and of Bengal and Assam in which the population is predominantly non-Muslim."

The possibility of a smaller "truncated" Pakistan confined to the Muslim majority areas alone was also considered. . . . "Such a Pakistan," it was stated, "is regarded by the Muslim League as quite impracticable.

We ourselves are also convinced that any solution which involves a radical partition of the Punjab and Bengal, as this would do, would be contrary to the wishes and interests of a very large proportion of the inhabitants of these Provinces. . . ."

Having rejected Pakistan, the Mission proceeded to expand and commend the scheme which had been discussed at Simla. In elaborating it they attempted to meet the views of both parties, but basically it remained the same. A three-tiered constitution was envisaged consisting of a Union limited to foreign affairs, defence and communications, Groups of Provinces dealing with such subjects as might later be determined, and the individual Provinces themselves in which all residuary powers would rest. After an initial period of ten years it was to be open to any Province, by a majority vote of its legislature, to call for a reconsideration of the constitution.

The Mission's statement then went on to propose that such a constitution should be brought into being by means of a Constituent Assembly to be elected by the members of the provincial legislatures, and that the Constituent Assembly should follow a certain procedure designed to meet Jinnah's objection to a single constitution-making body. It was proposed after an initial full meeting of a formal character, the Assembly should divide up into three sections — Section A consisting of the representatives of the five Hindu-majority provinces; Section B of the representatives of the Punjab, N.W.F.P. and Sind, and Section C of the representatives of Bengal and Assam. These Sections would draw up constitutions for the Provinces included in each of them and would also decide whether a group should be formed and if so with what subjects; but a Province would have the right to opt out of a group by a vote of its legislature *after* the new constitutional arrangements had come into operation. Finally the Constituent Assembly would meet again as a whole to settle the Union Constitution.

The statement referred to the need,

while the constitution-making proceeded, for an Interim Government in which all the portfolios would be held by Indian leaders having the confidence of the people. It was mentioned that the Viceroy had already started discussions to this end.

The statement was well received. It was recognized at once as a genuine and ingenious attempt to reconcile conflicting aims and as unmistakable evidence of the British Government's sincere desire to bring British rule in India to a peaceful end. Gandhi speaking at a prayer meeting on May 17th said that the Cabinet Mission had brought forth something of which they had every reason to be proud; and even ten days later, when doubts had begun to assail him, he still considered it "the best document the British Government could have produced in the circumstances." In spite of these encomiums it soon became clear that Gandhi and the Working Committee of Congress would scrutinize every line and comma of the statement before committing themselves to an acceptance of the proposals.

Jinnah was less enthusiastic. The statement had flatly rejected the idea of a sovereign, independent Pakistan, and this he could hardly be expected to applaud. But though outwardly more critical of the statement, he was really, as it proved, less inclined to cavil at it than Congress.

The largest volume of vocal opposition came from various minority groups who felt that their interests were not adequately safeguarded — and not least from the Sikhs. . . .

Meanwhile both the two major parties were examining the scheme, apparently with some disposition to accept it. Hopes of a settlement were enormously raised when on June 6th Jinnah, abandoning his usual negative attitude, got the Muslim League to pass a resolution accepting the scheme and agreeing to join the constitution-making body. The acceptance, it is true, was stated to be "in the hope that it would ultimately result in the establishment of complete sovereign Pakistan," which still remained the unalterable ob-

jective of the Muslims in India. But the Mission's scheme, whatever ultimate prospects and potentialities it might hold, was a definite rejection of "sovereign Pakistan." To have induced Jinnah at last publicly to accept something substantially less than what he had hitherto invariably demanded was a considerable success.

Jinnah's acceptance of the scheme had been fairly prompt and was certainly genuine; but it would be wrong to conclude that he agreed to it with enthusiasm. He had many misgivings and hesitated a good deal before recommending it to the Council of the League. Nevertheless from the Muslim point of view it offered solid advantages. . . .

But the prospects of agreement still hung in the balance. The Congress Working Committee had not given their verdict on the scheme and perhaps Jinnah's acceptance of it made them wish to scan it all the more closely. . . .

Days passed and the Congress Working Committee gave no decision but withdrew to Mussouri for recess, taking Gandhi with them. Meanwhile the Viceroy's attempts to bring about agreement between the two parties over the formation of an Interim Government had run up against the usual difficulties. The League claimed "parity" with Congress and the exclusive right to nominate Muslims. Congress rejected both these claims. It became clear that, as in the case of the constitutional problem, there was no prospect of negotiating an agreement between the parties and that the only course was for the Viceroy and the Mission to put forward their own proposals and hope that they would be accepted by both parties as a reasonable compromise. The Mission was also getting impatient to return home and desired to bring matters to a head. Accordingly on June 16th — before Congress had pronounced on the constitutional scheme — the Viceroy, in consultation with the members of the Mission, announced that further negotiations were being abandoned and that he had issued invitations to a named list of fourteen persons to serve as members of an Interim Government. These consisted of six Hindu members of Congress (including one member of the scheduled castes), five members of the Muslim League, öne Sikh, one Parsee and one Indian Christian. Thus Jinnah's claim to parity with Congress and with the Hindus was rejected, but his desire to veto non-League Muslims was respected.

The announcement stated that if the invitations were accepted by the two major parties it was hoped to inaugurate the new Government about June 26th. . . .

For a few days there was no public reaction to the announcement by either of the two major parties. The members of the Congress Working Committee had not all reassembled in Delhi and Gandhi also was temporarily absent. There was, however, a growing feeling of optimism. It was known that the proposals were acceptable to Jinnah; but he did not intend to intimate this until after Congress had spoken. In Congress circles there was some desire to substitute a Congress Muslim for one of the Congress Hindus, but it was hoped that they would not press the point in view of Jinnah's strong objection. Both Jawaharlal Nehru and Sardar Vallabhai Patel were believed to be in favour of acceptance and the rumour spread that the Congress Working Committee were going to express their readiness to work both the long-term and the short-term plan. All the labours of the past weeks — the endless discussions in the sweltering heat, the skilful and patient elaboration of a plan to suit all parties, the drafting and redrafting of statements and formulas — seemed on the point of being richly rewarded. For nine years Congress and the League had been engaged in barren controversy and non-co-operation. Now both were being successfully shepherded into a Coalition Government and into a Constituent Assembly which would frame a constitution on an agreed basis. A cartoon appeared in the *Hindustan Times* showing the Mission packing up to go home under the caption, "All's well that ends well."

It seemed too good to be true. And it was; for Gandhi had not been reckoned with. Once again at the critical moment he arrived on the scene and intervened with decisive and disastrous effect. Those who were inclined to acquiesce in the omission of a Congress Muslim from the Interim Government were overborne. Congress, being a national party with a Muslim president, could not, in Gandhi's view, agree to such an omission even as a temporary expedient and on the Viceroy's assurance that it would not be a precedent. It involved a principle that Congress could not give up. It mattered not that the principle had ceased to have practical significance now that Jinnah had won almost all the Muslims to his side. It mattered not that insistence on it would infuriate Jinnah, whose co-operation in any unitary form of government was essential, and would disrupt, with unpredictable consequences, the delicate web of negotiations spun by the Cabinet Mission. Such mundane and commonsense considerations did not appeal to Gandhi.

When the news spread that Congress were going to reject the proposals for an Interim Government the dismay in Cabinet Mission circles was intense, and intense too the indignation against Gandhi. It was he who had wrecked the Cripps Mission in 1942. Now he has done it again! Under the first shock of disappointment deliberate maleficence was attributed to him. This, of course, was mistaken. His influence may have been baleful, but it was not intended to be so. His advice may have been unwise, unstatesmanlike and, from the point of view of preserving India's unity, absolutely calamitous, but it was given in good faith and with the best of motives. If he could have been shown all the grim consequences that were to flow from it he would perhaps have said, as he had said on a previous occasion, that he had not the remotest idea of any such catastrophe resulting from it. Following the promptings of an inner voice he was all too often careless of consequences — until they overtook him. In this case they were to overtake him with a vengeance!

With the rejection of the short-term proposals by Congress the last chance of an agreement which might have averted partition was thrown away. This is clear now; but it was not fully apparent at the time; for hope revived when it became known that Congress, while rejecting the proposals for an Interim Government, had at last made up their minds to accept the long-term constitutional proposals. Something, at least, seemed to have been secured.

The acceptance when it came was qualified and ambiguous. It was conveyed in a long letter dated June 25th from the President, Maulana Abul Kalam Azad, to the Viceroy. "We have pointed out," the letter ran, "what in our opinion were the defects of the proposals. We also gave our interpretation of some of the provisions of the statement" — which the Mission had firmly repudiated. "While adhering to our views we accept your proposals and are prepared to work them with a view to achieve our objective."

This might mean . . . that they accepted the proposals only on *their* interpretation of them. But the Mission in their distress and disappointment were prepared to clutch at any convenient straws. This ambiguous acceptance, if not too closely scanned, gave ground for hope. . . . Treating, therefore, the Congress's decision as a real acceptance, they came out with a statement on June 26th expressing their happiness that "constitution-making can now proceed with the consent of the two major parties." The failure to form an Interim Government was, they said, regrettable; but, after a short interval, renewed efforts would be made by the Viceroy to bring such a Government into being "in accordance with . . . the statement of June 16th." They themselves would leave India on June 29th.

The few days before their departure were filled with acrimonious controversy. Jinnah, as soon as he knew that Congress had rejected the proposals for an Interim Government, had quickly got the Working Committee of the League to accept them. He then claimed, with some apparent justification, that the Viceroy was bound by . . . the statement of June 16th to ignore the Congress and proceed at once to form a government with representatives of the League and of such other parties as were willing to join. The plea that as both major parties had accepted the statement of May 16th, negotiations for an Interim Government has to be taken up *de novo,* had been dishonestly concocted by the legalistic talents of the Cabinet Mission. He roundly charged the Viceroy and the Mission with breach of faith and cuttingly observed: "Statesmen should not eat their words."

So the Mission ended in disappointment tinged with resentment; for it was to the accompaniment of Jinnah's taunts and reproaches that the three Cabinet Ministers took their departure. This public controversy belied the hopes expressed that constitution-making would go forward speedily in a spirit of accommodation. . . .

Within a fortnight of the Mission's departure all that remained of their precarious card-house had collapsed in irretrievable ruin. Gandhi, by persuading the Working Committee to reject the interim proposals, had already knocked down half of it. Nehru now proceeded to demolish the rest. At a press conference on July 10th he said that Congress, in accepting the Cabinet Mission's long-term plan, "have agreed to go into the Constituent Assembly and have agreed to nothing else . . . we have committed ourselves to no single matter to anybody." Thus the basic structure of the constitution, including the strict limitation of federal subjects, and the procedure to be followed by the Constituent Assembly, all of which formed part of the long-term proposals ostensibly accepted by Congress, had in reality not been accepted at all. In regard to grouping, which the Mission had specifically stated to be an essential feature of their plan, Nehru expressed the view that "the big probability is that . . . there will be no grouping." The reasons which he gave showed complete disregard for the Cabinet Mission's intentions as to the manner of voting in the Sections. Contemptuously brushing the Mission aside he declared that what they thought or intended did not enter into the matter at all!

Jinnah retorted at once, and with some justice, that Nehru's interpretation of the acceptance as amounting to nothing more than an agreement to go into the Constituent Assembly was a "complete repudiation of the basic form upon which the long-term scheme rests and all its fundamentals and terms and obligations." It was clear, he said, that the Congress's so-called "acceptance" of the long-term plan had been from the outset disingenuous — they had never intended to honour it. Since this was their attitude, since they did not really intend to abide by the plan or to work it in a spirit of compromise and co-operation, but rather to use their majority in the Constituent Assembly to enforce their own views, the Muslim League would have to reconsider the situation.

This they did at the end of the month. At a meeting held in Bombay they decided to withdraw their previous acceptance of the long-term plan and to prepare a programme of "direct action" for the achievement of Pakistan to be launched as and when necessary. "This day," Jinnah announced, "we bid goodbye to constitutional methods."

Nothing was now left of the Cabinet Mission's fragile edifice and, try as he might over the next six months, Lord Wavell was unable to reconstruct it. Congress could not be brought to declare unequivocally their acceptance of the long-term proposals in the sense that the League understood them and the Cabinet Mission had intended them; while Jinnah and the League would be content with nothing less. There was thus no agreed basis for constitution-making and hence no prospect of co-operation. There had never in reality been any agreement at all, but only the illusion of one.

The League's withdrawal of their accept-

ance of the long-term plan, though it meant that they would take no part in the Constituent Assembly, simplified in some ways the formation of an Interim Government. It was decided, though with a good deal of misgiving, to go ahead without them, and accordingly on August 6th the Viceroy wrote to Nehru — who had recently succeeded Azad as Congress President — inviting him to form a government. The invitation was accepted.

Before the new government had taken office or the names of its members had been announced, the first fruits of the Cabinet Mission's failure were being gathered. On August 16th, which the Muslim League celebrated as "Direct Action Day," there was an appalling outbreak of rioting in Calcutta, lasting several days. According to official estimates about 5,000 persons were killed and 15,000 injured. Compared with what was to follow this holocaust was nothing extraordinary, but it made a deep impression at the time. People had not yet become hardened to mass slaughter. . . .

The Viceroy thought that the dangers of the situation would be lessened if the League could be brought into the Interim Government. He also had reason to believe that the League would once again accept the long-term proposals and enter the Constituent Assembly if Congress would unequivocally agree to grouping as contemplated in the statement of May 16th. He strove hard to bring the two parties to terms and his efforts seemed partially successful when in the middle of October Jinnah agreed that five nominees of the League should join the Government. They took office on October 26th. . . .

But it soon became apparent that Jinnah's assurances were of no value. The League had entered the Government not to co-operate with Congress but simply to prevent Congress from tightening its hold on the whole governmental machine at the League's expense. The Interim Government became in fact a dual government. There was, as Liaquat Ali Khan put it, "a Congress bloc and a Muslim bloc, each functioning under separate leadership." Each began to attract to itself its own supporters from among the civil servants and to build up its own separate and exclusive empire. As a Coalition Government it was a farce.

There was also no progress in regard to the League's entry into the Constituent Assembly. . . .

A dangerous crisis was now approaching. . . .

If the Congress members withdrew [from the Interim Government], the British, with League support, might have to hold down forcibly the whole of Hindu India. On the other hand the extrusion of the League representatives from the Central Government would be the signal for fresh communal disorders which might lead to a virtual state of civil war; for there was a danger now that the army and services would begin to take sides. The British Government would then be compelled either to restore order by British arms — and this would involve reassertion of British dominance for at least ten to fifteen years — or to scuttle ignominiously from the anarchic situation.

Physically the reassertion of British authority would not have been very difficult; but politically and psychologically it was quite impracticable — neither British opinion nor world opinion would have tolerated it or permitted the necessary measures to be taken. The Labour Government rightly ruled it out. But some fresh move had to be made. Drift and delay could only lead to chaos. So they took a bold decision. On February 20th the Prime Minister, Mr. Attlee, announced in the House of Commons that it was His Majesty's Government's "definite intention to take the necessary steps to effect the transference of power to responsible Indian hands by a date not later than June 1948." All parties were urged to sink their differences — it was no doubt hoped that the mere fixing of a date so close at hand would shock them into some kind of agreement — but lack of agreement would not cause any postponement of the date. If it appeared by the date

fixed a fully representative Constituent Assembly would not have worked out a constitution in accordance with the Cabinet Mission's proposals, His Majesty's Government would have to consider

to whom the powers of the Central Government in British India should be handed over, on the due date, whether as a whole to some form of Central Government for British India, or in some areas to the existing Provincial Governments, or in such other way as may seem most reasonable and in the best interests of the Indian people.

This announcement meant Partition, and Partition within the next seventeen months. Whatever London might think, everyone in Delhi knew that the Cabinet Mission's proposals were as dead as mutton. No constitution would be framed on their basis; and owing to the Hindu-Muslim feud there would be no Central Government capable of exercising authority over the whole of British India to whom the powers of the existing Government of India could be transferred. The power which the British held would have to be divided in order to be demitted, as indeed Mr. Attlee's statement itself vaguely foreshadowed. The British Government and Gandhi might perhaps still delude themselves with the hope of a united independent India; but for others it had faded from sight. As Sir Seyed Ahmad had foreseen years earlier, two nations — Muslim and Hindu — could not sit on the same throne.

Thus nine months of strenuous British endeavour to preserve unity had led only to the inevitability of Partition. This deplorable outcome is not attributable . . . simply or even mainly to Gandhi's ill-starred interventions or Nehru's fits of arrogant impatience. At critical moments they may have given an adverse turn to events and thereby occasioned a result which neither of them desired. But the reasons for the failure to agree on some form of united India lay deeper. The truth is that the aims and aspirations of the two communities, as expressed by those whom they acclaimed their leaders, were irreconcilable; and, as it turned out in the end, their professed aims were also their real ones. The Congress leaders wanted a strong united India; the League a divided or divisible one. The Congress aim had never been in doubt and accurately reflected the wishes of the Hindu community. The League's aim, only proclaimed in 1940, may not have reflected any real or rational wish of the Muslim multitude, but at least accorded with their blind impulses. Instinctively they had rallied to Jinnah, deserting other leaders; and Jinnah, whatever his original views, had by now, rightly or wrongly, come to regard "a sovereign independent Pakistan," actual or at least permanently potential, as an indispensable Muslim need.

This deep difference of aim could not be bridged by a flimsy paper scheme, such as the Cabinet Mission had devised. Both parties, in so far as they accepted it at all, avowedly did so in order to achieve their own objectives — and these were contradictory. This being so, even if constitution-making had begun, it could hardly have got very far; and even if a constitution, such as the Cabinet Mission envisaged, had somehow come into being, it could hardly have worked for very long.

IV. IN RETROSPECT

Partition Should Have Been Postponed

MAULANA AZAD

As the following passages from his autobiography show, Maulana Azad
as late as 1947 believed that partition was not inevitable, nor did he deem it a
satisfactory solution for India's problems. The British Labour Prime Minister had
argued that the date for British withdrawal should be quickly and unequivocally
fixed. The Viceroy, Lord Wavell, demurred. He argued that precipitous departure would likely bring violence and that the status quo should be maintained until some semblance of agreements could be secured from the antagonistic parties. Azad is inclined to believe that Wavell was right, and that much
more effort should have been expended in trying to avoid what Azad believed
was an unmitigated tragedy.

THE Labour Government in Britain felt that they were faced with a dilemma. Should they allow the present state to continue or should they take a forward step on their own initiative? Mr. Attlee was of the view that a stage had been reached where suspense was most undesirable. It was necessary to take a clear-cut decision and he decided that the British Government should fix a date for the withdrawal of British power from India. Lord Wavell did not agree regarding the announcement of a date. He wished to persist with the Cabinet Mission Plan, for he held that it was the only possible solution of the Indian problem. He further held that the British Government would fail in its duty if it transferred political power before the communal question had been solved. Passions had been roused to such a peak in India that even responsible people were carried away. The withdrawal of British power in such an atmosphere would in his view lead to widespread riots and disturbances. He therefore advised that the *status quo* should be maintained and that every attempt should be made to compose the difference between the two major parties. It was his firm conviction that it would be dangerous and unworthy if the British withdrew without a previous understanding between Congress and the League.

Mr. Attlee did not agree. He held that once a dateline was fixed, the responsibility would be transferred to Indian hands. Unless this was done, there would never be any solution. Mr. Attlee feared that if the *status quo* was continued, Indians would lose their faith in the British Government. Conditions in India were such that the British could not maintain their power without an effort which the British people

From Maulana Azad, *India Wins Freedom* (Bombay: Orient Longmans Ltd.) pp. 177–178, 226.
Reprinted by permission of Orient Longmans Ltd.

were not prepared to make. The only alternatives were to rule with a firm hand and suppress all disturbances, or transfer power to the Indians themselves. The Government could continue to govern, but this would require an effort which would interfere with the reconstruction of Britain. The other alternative was to fix a date for the transfer of power and thus place the responsibility squarely on Indian shoulders.

Lord Wavell was not convinced. He still argued that if communal difficulties led to violence, history would not forgive the British. The British had governed India for over a hundred years and they would be responsible if unrest, violence and disorder broke out as a result of their withdrawal. When he found that he could not convince Mr. Attlee, Lord Wavell offered his resignation.

Looking at the events after ten years, I sometimes wonder who was right. The circumstances were so complicated and the situation so delicate that it is difficult to give a clear judgment. Mr. Attlee's decision was governed by his determination to help India to attain independence. Anyone with the slightest imperialist tendencies could easily have exploited India's weakness. In fact, Hindu-Muslim differences had always been exploited by the British Government. This had been their supreme defence against the Indian demand for independence. Mr. Attlee was resolved that the Labour Government should not adopt any policy which would lay it open to such a charge.

We must admit that if his motives had not been pure and if he had wished to exploit the differences between Congress and the League he could easily have done so. In spite of our opposition the British could have governed this country for another decade. There would of course have been disturbances and clashes. Indian feelings had been aroused to a level where British rule would have been challenged at every step. Nevertheless they could have, if they had so wished, continued to rule for a few

more years by exploiting Indian differences. We must not forget that the French continued in Indo-China for almost ten years, even though France was much weaker than Britain. We must therefore give due credit to the motives of the Labour Government. They did not wish to exploit Indian weakness for their own advantage. History will honour them for this judgment and we must also without any mental reservation acknowledge this fact.

On the other hand, one cannot say for certain that Lord Wavell was wrong. The dangers he foresaw were real and later events proved that his reading of the situation was not incorrect. It is difficult to say which of the alternatives — the one actually adopted by Mr. Attlee or the one suggested by Lord Wavell — would have been better for India. If Lord Wavell's advice had been followed and the solution of the Indian problem deferred for a year or two, it is possible that the Muslim League would have got tired of its opposition. Even if the League had not taken a more positive attitude, the Muslim masses of India would probably have repudiated the negative attitude of the Muslim League. It is even possible that the tragedy of Indian partition might have been avoided. One cannot say for certain, but a year or two is nothing in the history of a nation. Perhaps history will decide that the wiser policy would have been to follow Lord Wavell's advice. . . .

In fact, the more I think about it the more I am convinced that the creation of Pakistan has solved no problem. One may argue that the relations between Hindus and Muslims had become so estranged in India that there was no alternative to partition. This view was held by most of the supporters of the Muslim League and after partition many of the Congress leaders have held a similar view. Whenever I discussed the question with Jawaharlal or Sardar Patel after partition, this was the argument they gave in support of their decision. If however we look the matter over coolly, we shall find that their analysis is not correct. I am convinced that the scheme I framed on the occasion of the Cabinet Mission and which the Mission largely accepted, was a far better solution from every point of view. If we had remained steadfast and refused to accept partition, I am confident that a safer and more glorious future would have awaited us.

Broken Faith and the Decision for Pakistan

I. H. QURESHI

Dr. I. H. Qureshi, Vice Chancellor of the University of Karachi, presents a contrasting view of the events of 1946–47 from that given in the previous selection by Maulana Azad. Azad was a "Nationalist" Muslim who believed that the future of Muslims was secure in an undivided India, and that Islamic interests would be better served by the acceptance of a secular democratic state rather than creating an Islamic one. Dr. Qureshi, an authority on the history of Islam in India, chose to go to Pakistan after 1947. In the book from which the following selection is taken he argued that much of "the terrible legacy of bitterness and hostility" might have been avoided, if the history of Islam in India had been taken seriously. The idea that the Muslims would accept the interpretation of nationalism stressed by the Indian National Congress was built, he wrote, "upon the most deplorable ignorance of the psychology of the Muslim community."

THE only Congressman who saw the necessity of arriving at some compromise was Rajagopalachari, who made a resolution in the All-India Congress Committee in May 1942 conceding the principle of Pakistan, but he was not able to carry it. So unpopular was this move that he had to resign from the Congress. When Gandhi was released in 1944, he was persuaded by Rajagopalachari to have discussions with Jinnah, but the talks proved abortive. Throughout, their arguments ran on parallel tracks without ever being able to establish any contact. In the spring of 1945 when Germany had been defeated, Lord Wavell, the viceroy, convened a conference at Simla in which he renewed the proposal regarding the expansion of the Executive Council; the conference proved unsuccessful because the Congress demanded the right to nominate a Congress Muslim and the viceroy wanted to give a seat to the unpopular Unionist Party of the Panjab out of the Muslim quota. Soon after, the war against Japan came to an end and at the same time Labour won the elections in the United Kingdom. New elections were ordered to test the claims of the various political parties in India; these elections completely vindicated Jinnah's claim that the Muslims were solidly behind the Muslim League, which captured all the Muslim seats in the Central Assembly and 446 out of 495 Muslim seats in the provincial assemblies. The main losses of the League were in the North-Western Frontier Province where 'Abd-u'l-Ghaffār Khān had considerable influence.

In March 1946 the British cabinet sent a mission of three members to evolve some method of framing a constitution for India. Their prolonged discussions with the different leaders produced no agreement, hence they produced a plan which is known as the Cabinet Mission Plan. It suggested the election of a constituent as-

From I. H. Qureshi, *The Muslim Community of the Indo-Pakistan Subcontinent* (The Hague, 1962), pp. 301–304. Reprinted by permission of Mouton & Co., n.v.

sembly to frame a constitution for a Union of India. Foreign Affairs, Defence and Communications would form the federal subjects. After a preliminary session the provincial delegates would meet in three sections. The first consisted of the region where the Hindus formed a majority; the second consisted of the Punjab, the North-Western Frontier Province, and Sind; the third of Bengal and Assam. In these sections the provincial delegates would decide whether they wanted to form a group for the common administration of certain provincial subjects. This plan was announced on 16 May 1946; a month after, on 16 June 1946, the viceroy, in consultation with the Cabinet Mission, issued a statement regarding the expansion of his cabinet, in which, *inter alia,* he said:

In the event of the two major parties or either of them proving unwilling to join in the setting up of a Coalition Government on the above lines, it is the intention of the Viceroy to proceed with the formation of an Interim Government which will be as representative as possible of those willing to accept the statement of May 16.

The League obtained an assurance from the viceroy that the government "shall go ahead with the plan, so far as circumstances permit, if either party accepts"; on 6 June it accepted the entire plan. On 26 June the Congress accepted the constitutional part of the plan but refused to join the interim government. At this the viceroy appointed a caretaker government consisting of officials and did not invite the League to form the government.

This was a clear breach of a solemn undertaking. It is true that the purpose of an interim government would not have been served if the Congress had been left out; but then such an undertaking should not have been given. It seems obvious from these transactions that the Cabinet Mission had expected the League to reject the plan because it did not concede full independence to the Muslim majority areas and, therefore, the condition of proceeding with

the formation of the interim government with the support of a single party had been incorporated with a view to leaving out the League if it proved obdurate; but Jinnah frustrated this attempt by his acceptance. There was great resentment among the Muslims; specially when, immediately after their acceptance of the constitutional part of the plan as well, Congress leaders had started putting their own interpretation upon the proposals which ran counter to the explanations given by the Cabinet Mission. The League now withdrew its acceptance of the proposals, called upon all Muslims to renounce their titles and decided to launch a campaign of Direct Action for the achievement of independent Pakistan. The Congress then entered the government and all the members of the Viceroy's Executive Council were the nominees of the Congress. The League soon felt that a government entirely in the hands of its opponents was detrimental to Muslim interests and, therefore, it also joined the government.

In the meanwhile elections to the Constituent Assembly had taken place and it began its work. The Muslim League members, however, did not attend. It was now realized both in Great Britain and in the Congress circles that a constitution framed by a body from which the Muslims were absent could not be imposed upon them. The result of this was that a new plan was announced on 3 June 1947 which brought Pakistan into existence.

It may be added here that there were among the Muslims a few leaders and some splinter groups that were not in favour of Partition. Of these perhaps the Jam'iyat-u'l-'ulamā was the most interesting, because one expected from their traditions that they would support the idea of the establishment of an independent Muslim state with enthusiasm. However the conservatism which has become so deeply ingrained in the system of theological studies in the subcontinent led them to think that the only right course would be the one which had been laid for them by Shaikh-u'l-Hind Mahmūd-u'l-Hasan, when he had participated in the Khilafat Movement and insisted upon unity with the Hindus. The handful of leaders who were still with the Congress were also mostly those who had developed a tradition of cooperating with the Congress before the movement of Pakistan came to the forefront. The rank and file among the Muslim community, as the election results in 1945 showed, enthusiastically supported the demand for Pakistan; the most enthusiastic supporters of the demand came from the provinces in which the Muslims formed a minority.

Observers of the growth of the Pakistan movement were surprised at the rapidity with which the idea spread among the Muslims. The emotional attachment to the ideal of Pakistan also grew in intensity as soon as it seemed that it was feasible to establish an independent Muslim state in the subcontinent. Anyone who has studied the desire of the Muslims of the subcontinent to maintain their separate identity throughout its history would understand the appeal of Pakistan to the community. Besides, since it lost political authority, the desire for a Muslim state has been deep-rooted in the consciousness of the community. On the negative side was the absence of cementing factors in the relations of the two communities. They have lived with minimum contacts; there has been little inter-marriage, because Islam forbids it with the Hindus and the Hindus are bound by their rules of caste; except in a small sector of the highly Westernized class, inter-dining has been unthinkable; the festivals provide no social occasion for coming together, instead they have often given a pretext for rioting; the communities have remained different not only in religion, but in everything, culture, thought, outlook on life, even in the fashions of dress, cookery, furniture and domestic utensils. More than anything else, there has been no sense of a common history; instead there are two views of such historical happenings as are capable of creating any emotion; the heroes of the Muslim conquest and the rebels against Muslim domination inspire contradictory feelings among the Muslims and the Hindus; common bondage to a foreign government also, as would appear from this narrative, did not always inspire the same feelings at all times; even if it had, more positive influences are needed in building up nations. The attitude of the Muslim community towards the idea of Pakistan was, therefore, the logical consequence of its history.

Subsequent developments belong more properly to the history of Pakistan. On 14 August 1947, when Pakistan came into existence, the place of the Muslim community of the subcontinent was taken by the Pakistani nation and the Muslim minority still living in the Indian Union. It is not the function of history to speculate about the pattern that will arise from this division.

A Failure of Statesmanship

PENDEREL MOON

Divide and Quit is one of the few books expressly concerned with partition. The author's analysis of the Cabinet Mission's proposals has already been presented earlier; in this excerpt he gives a capsule explanation of the events of 1947. Moon asserts that up to 1937 Pakistan could easily have been avoided. This may be an over-optimistic view of Indian history but he next proceeds to argue that the period from 1937 to 1942 was decisive. After the failure of the Cripps Mission and the failure of Congress to cooperate in the war effort, little could be done to avert Indian bifurcation. One of the significant points made by the author refers to Jinnah's desertion of Congress and his deep distrust of the emotional, semireligious appeal of Gandhi. Partition, at least its seeds, was sown with the Mahatma's civil disobedience campaigns of the 1920's. Despite Gandhi's claim of universality and tolerance in the religious sphere, he was "preeminently a Hindu," and Congress "an essentially Hindu institution."

I N THIS narrative the course of events leading to the creation of Pakistan has been traced only from the year 1937; for though Pakistan had its roots much further back in history, as is apparent from the ideas expressed by Sir Seyed Ahmad in the nineteenth century, it was only after 1937 that it became a live political issue. I propose, therefore, to examine whether its avoidance was possible only from 1937 onwards and not to dig down deeply into the events of an earlier period. As regards pre-1937, I will dwell only on one significant fact, namely that Gandhi's rise to ascendancy in Congress was more or less coincident with Jinnah's estrangement from it.

In 1917 Jinnah was a member and keen supporter of Congress, noted primarily as an Indian rather than a purely Muslim nationalist. At that time he was pooh-poohing the threat of Hindu domination. "Fear not," he said, "this is a bogy which is put before you to scare you away from the co-operation and unity which are essential to self-government." So long as Congress was led by men like G. K. Gokhale, who spoke the familiar language of Western liberalism and constitutionalism, Jinnah felt at home in it. But the growing influence of Gandhi at the end of World War I set it on unconstitutional paths and simultaneously gave it a more pronounced Hindu complexion. To these developments Jinnah could not reconcile himself. He parted from Congress in 1928.

Jinnah's dislike of Gandhi — that "Hindu revivalist" as he called him — was deep-seated; and he distrusted profoundly his methods of non-co-operation and organized agitation. They "have already caused split and division," he wrote to him in 1920, "in almost every institution that you have approached hitherto," and he predicted that they would "lead to disaster" —

From Penderel Moon, *Divide and Quit* (London, 1961), pp. 270–274, 282–290. Reprinted by permission of Chatto & Windus Ltd. and the University of California Press.

as indeed they did as regards Hindu-Muslim unity, the preservation of which was an objective which at that time both of them shared. The fact is — as Jinnah seems dimly to have perceived — that with Gandhi's decision not to co-operate with the British and to launch a campaign of civil disobedience the seeds of separation were being sown. Civil disobedience involved an appeal to the masses, and an appeal to the masses by an organization headed and symbolized by Gandhi was necessarily an emotional, semi-religious appeal to the Hindu masses and not to the Muslims; for Gandhi with all his fads and fastings, his goat's milk, mud baths, days of silence and fetish of non-violence was pre-eminently a Hindu. He himself claimed to be "a Muslim, a Hindu, a Buddhist, a Christian, a Jew, a Parsee." But this claim did not cut much ice; indeed who but a Hindu could entertain such a preposterous hope of being all things to all men?

Gandhian leadership of Congress was highly successful in securing for the nationalist movement popular backing from the Hindus; and popular backing was considered necessary in order to bring pressure on the British to relax their hold on India. Whether this view was correct is open to question. It may well be that the British could have been induced to leave just as quickly if Congress had stuck to strictly constitutional methods and had consistently co-operated with the British instead of doing the reverse. However this may be, under Gandhi's leadership Congress took the opposite course and, instead of remaining just an organization of the intelligentsia, deliberately sought to enlist wide support. But to appeal to the masses was to run the risk of rousing the latent Hindu-Muslim antagonism that existed at mass level. Congress, it is true, achieved in the N.W.F.P. a limited and deceptive success among the Muslim masses, and it continued to enjoy the support of a few distinguished Muslim intellectuals. But in general the more Gandhi became the idol of the Congress and the more Congress diffused itself among the masses, the more the Muslims as a whole stood aloof from it, viewing it coldly as an essentially Hindu institution.

The danger that his methods would provoke Muslim antipathy was not adequately appreciated by Gandhi who, with the normal Hindu tendency to prefer dreams to facts, ideals to reality, could not divest himself of the belief that Congress — more particularly Congress as personified by himself — could and did represent everybody, or at any rate everybody that mattered. This fatal self-deception had already by 1937 done serious, though not irreparable, damage to the cause of national unity. What was ultimately to prove worse, Gandhian policies had also alienated Jinnah who instead of being friendly to Congress was by now potentially, though not as yet actually, hostile. No one, of course, could have foreseen that he would prove such an implacable foe. Unknowingly, however, Gandhi had helped to transform him from a keen nationalist into the chief architect of Pakistan.

At the beginning of 1937 all this was still in the womb of time. Jinnah had no considerable following and his prospective importance was not at all apparent. The question "Can Pakistan be avoided?" could hardly have been asked, since Pakistan was not yet envisaged as even a remote possibility. Though Hindu-Muslim differences were fairly acute, even Jinnah and the League had not suggested that division of the country was an appropriate or possible solution of them. At this stage Pakistan was still quite easily avoidable. When were the mistakes made which caused it in a few years to become absolutely unavoidable?

When a boat is being carried downstream by the current of a river towards a weir or dangerous rapids, it is difficult to fix the precise moment at which all efforts to save it become vain and nothing can prevent it from being swept to disaster. At a distance from the fall the rowers, if they realize in time the danger ahead of them and exert themselves, will be strong enough to make head against the current. Even if they neglect this opportunity and let the boat drift down to where the current is too much for them, there may still be time to steer it to the safety of the bank. But there comes a point, not exactly identifiable, when the force of the current will take complete charge and draw the boat irresistibly to destruction.

So it was with Pakistan. In 1938 the current making for it was quite discernible, but was not yet too strong to be resisted. By 1942 it had gained tremendously in strength, but there still seemed to be ways of avoiding its worst effects. Even as late as 1946 it appeared at the time that there was a slender chance of steering clear of an absolute division of the country. By the end of that year division was seen to be inevitable.

The crucial years were 1937–42. It was in this period that mistakes were committed and opportunities let slip which made unavailing the later efforts to avoid the division of the country. First came the Congress's mistake of declining to form coalition governments with the League in those Provinces in which they had a majority. The mistake was very natural, perhaps unavoidable, and by no means fatal. It could have been retrieved. But Congress did not perceive the importance of retrieving it because they did not appreciate how deep and widespread were the fears which it had aroused among the Muslim intelligentsia. Yet they had sufficient warning. The immediate rallying of all Muslims to the League banner and the doubts which Muslims began to express about submitting to a permanent Hindu majority at the Centre were very plain danger signals. Congress did not read them.

The outbreak of war afforded a splendid opportunity of repairing the damage that had been done. On the plea of a national emergency Congress could have retraced their steps and sought to join with the League in coalitions both in the Provinces and at the Centre. If Congress had entered into such working partnerships with the League while moderate men were still in control of the Muslim masses both in Bengal and the Punjab, the forces of disruption could have been checked. But Congress elected to follow the barren path of non-co-operation — non-co-operation with both the British and the League — and resigned office in all the provinces in which they held it.

From the point of view of preserving Indian unity, this was perhaps the most foolish step Congress ever took. In fairness it must be said that several Congress leaders consented to it with reluctance and misgiving; and Gandhi's own initial instinct was against it. If the British had shown more generosity and imagination the scales might have been tipped the other way. But the chance was missed and Congress, blind to the importance of reaching accommodation with the Muslims while there was yet time and obsessed by their struggle with the British, gave up office and with it the prospect of coalitions with the League. Within six months Jinnah and the League had committed themselves to the demand for Pakistan.

In so far as Jinnah really wanted Pakistan, despite all the calamities which it would necessarily entail, he cannot be held to have been guilty of a mistake in demanding it in 1940. If, however, as seems probable, he did not at this stage really intend to follow the demand through to its logical conclusion, then it was a grave — a criminal — error to raise such a dangerous slogan, and Sikander, who clearly foresaw the dangers, was also much to blame for weakly consenting to it. If they were unable to dissuade Jinnah from his course, they should have broken with him at this time instead of giving their tacit blessing to a demand for the absolute division of the country.

Probably the last chance of averting an absolute division came in 1942 with the "Cripps" offer. If it had been accepted,

Congress and the League would at any rate have participated together in the defence of India against the Japanese and the partnership might have prevented an absolute break later. The chance was not taken.

After this all further rescue operations were probably vain. It seemed at the time that the Cabinet Missions of 1946 had an outside chance of saving the unity of India and that this was thrown away through the bad judgement first of Gandhi and then of Nehru. In retrospect this chance appears to have been illusory. The constitution-making machinery proposed by the Cabinet Mission might have been brought into operation, if it had not been for the mistakes of the Congress leaders; but it could hardly have produced an agreed constitution for a single Indian Union. Congress and the League were by this time such poles apart, so much the slaves of their own slogans and animosities, so much imbued with mutual hostility and distrust that the Constituent Assembly as envisaged by the Cabinet Mission, if it had ever started to function, would have broken up in confusion and strife.

To sum up: A general lack of wisdom and statesmanship in the years 1937–42 made Pakistan unavoidable. Thereafter British efforts to preserve the unity of India were sincere and well-conceived — it is difficult to see what more they could have done — but passions had been too deeply aroused for human reason to control the course of events. . . .

Postponement of Partition by ten months could have done no good; and it carried with it dangers of its own. Sparks from suppressed fires in the Punjab were liable to ignite combustible materials in other parts of India. Any delay in separating the armed forces might give occasion, in the excited state of feeling, for clashes between Muslim and non-Muslim units with incalculable consequences. The three parties who had agreed to the Mountbatten plan might resile from it, if they were given too much time for reflection. Furthermore, from the purely British point of view there was

the danger that the drastic measures which would be necessary for keeping the peace in the Punjab would earn them the odium of all three communities and that they would in the end leave the country amid general execration.

All things considered, it must really be accounted a mercy that Lord Mountbatten did not foresee more clearly the magnitude of the calamity that threatened the Punjab. Had he done so, he might have fumbled and faltered, casting about vainly for means of avoiding it while the country drifted into civil war. As it was, by driving ahead at top speed with his plan for Partition he successfully divided the country and the armed forces before they could be engulfed in universal strife, and the Punjab alone had to pay in blood the price of freedom.

While Lord Mountbatten may be absolved from blame, the claim, often put forward, to great merit for the manner of our departure from India rings somewhat hollow. It is true that the disturbances of 1947 were more or less confined to the north-west of the sub-continent and that the tribulations of the Punjab meant no more to central and southern India than did the horrors of the Spanish civil war to the rest of Europe. Yet that the ending of the British Raj, which we had so long foreseen and so long proclaimed as our goal, should involve a last-minute division of the country which we had ourselves united, the sudden rending in twain of two large well-knit provinces, the precipitate, enforced migration of well over ten million people, and casualties of the order of 200,000 does seem to argue a singular want of prevision and failure of statesmanship.

For this the British bear a good share of the responsibility. The complacency shown by them from 1937 to 1942, when the demand for Pakistan was first gathering strength, has been commented upon in earlier chapters. It is possible, though by no means certain, that if from the outset the British had made it quite clear that they would never countenance Pakistan, the division of the country would have been avoided. But it was very difficult, if not impossible, for them to do this. By the time the demand for Pakistan was actually put forward by the Muslim League, World War II had already broken out and the main Hindu political organization, Congress, was standing aloof in an attitude of passive hostility. In these circumstances the British could hardly have been expected to risk antagonizing also the principal Muslim political party by turning down their demand out of hand. They were also precluded from doing so by the repeated assurances given earlier that the wishes and interests of the minorities would not be lightly overridden. The most, therefore, that the British could do at this time was to temporize and to use their best endeavours to bridge the chasm that had opened between Congress and the League. The latter they certainly failed to do in the period 1937 to 1942.

But to understand fully the British responsibility one has to go back further. The root of the trouble lay in the decision to introduce parliamentary democracy into a society which was far from homogeneous and riven with the deep Hindu-Muslim cleavage. The irrevocable step was taken with the Montagu-Chelmsford reforms at the end of World War I. Ten years earlier the liberal Secretary of State, Lord Morley, when introducing his own Morley-Minto reforms, had said that he would have nothing to do with reforms which directly or necessarily led to the establishment of a parliamentary system in India. But by 1919 the tide running in favour of parliamentary democracy was too strong to be resisted. Almost everywhere sceptres and crowns were tumbling down and being replaced by democratic institutions. The Indian intelligentsia, deeply imbued with the ideas of English liberalism, could not think of freedom from foreign rule in any other terms; and even English opinion, lacking for the most part any real insight into Indian conditions, tended to view with equanimity, if not enthusiasm, the export of parliamentary democracy to India. And so there was introduced into a vast country of illiterate peasants, belonging to diverse races and religions and held together only by geography and common subjection to British rule, a system of government which, while it has served the English and some closely kindred peoples well enough, has elsewhere been — and doubtless will continue to be — a constant source of strife, disunity and disruption.

The inherent dangers of this British-sponsored experiment would have been lessened if the British, having once launched it, had hastened to transfer all political power to Indian hands before the constant appeals to the gallery inseparable from democratic processes had time to inflame feelings and accentuate the Hindu-Muslim division. But the British, fighting a stubborn rearguard action, conceded power in the inter-war period only slowly and reluctantly. While it is not true, as is often alleged against them, that in this period they deliberately promoted divisions, they certainly took advantage of the divisions that existed in order to justify the prolongation of their rule, and they failed, until quite near the end, actively to promote unity. Their hesitation to part with power in the inter-war period gave time for the communal situation to deteriorate and the cry of Pakistan to be raised. If in 1929, when the Montagu-Chelmsford reforms came up for review, they had boldly decided to treat Dominion Status as an immediate and not a distant objective and had set about with some determination to frame a constitution on this basis with merely a few transitional safeguards, then by the early thirties a Central Government representative of the major Hindu and Muslim parties would have been installed in power before anyone had occasion to think of Partition. And once the country had virtually reached the goal of independence as a unity, that unity would have been preserved at least for some time; for, apart from the bias of sheer inertia in favor of the status quo, the Muslims of the Muslim-majority provinces, with wide control over their provincial affairs, would have had no strong motive for secession. What might ultimately have been the outcome is a matter of speculation, but at least the British would have brought their rule in India to a blameless close.

If therefore the British ever care to ask wherein lay their responsibility for the massacres and migrations of 1947, the answer may be succinctly given. It lay in their belief in the virtues of parliamentary democracy and their reluctance to part with power.

Responsibility did not rest only with the British. Countless Indians and Pakistanis of every walk of life share the guilt for these events. . . . I inquired the truth of the matter from a friend on the Indian side. . . . He . . . went on to point out that he and many others like him were largely the victims of circumstances and that real responsibility rested higher up and ultimately, and in greatest measure, on two persons — Gandhi and Jinnah.

Jinnah's responsibility is the more obvious and was certainly the more deliberate. It is a measure of his guilt, but also of his greatness, that without him Pakistan would never have come into being. His career affords a striking illustration of the influence of a single individual — and also of sheer chance — on the broad course of history. Only Jinnah, and none of his lieutenants whether singly or combined, could have mastered all the Muslims of the Punjab and Bengal, dominating or overthrowing their own leaders, and swung them in favour of a policy and objective to which they were originally opposed. Yet Jinnah would never have had the opportunity to seize the lead and make Pakistan the goal of all the Muslims had it not been for the accident of fate which removed from the scene in 1936 the great Punjabi Muslim, Sir Fazl-i-Husain, at the comparatively early age of fifty-nine. Sir Fazli was the founder of the Unionist Party, a staunch Muslim, a staunch Punjabi, but also a staunch Nationalist. Like Jinnah he was a man of integrity, and in ability, force of character and renown he was more than his equal. If he had lived to lead the Unionist Party for another ten years instead of dying prematurely and giving place to lesser men, Jinnah would not have been able, and would not even have attempted, to win over the allegiance of the Punjabi Muslims and Pakistan would have remained an "impracticable students' scheme." But fate decreed otherwise and by removing Sir Fazli gave Jinnah his chance.

The responsibility for first putting forward "Pakistan" as the well-nigh unanimous demand of the Muslims rests squarely on Jinnah. It was he who, despite the misgivings of Sir Sikander and many others, transformed it from an esoteric fancy into a powerful political slogan. Even if originally he made the demand only as a tactical move, he stuck to it thereafter so uncompromisingly — only at the time of the Cabinet Missions showing a disposition to accept something less — that a settlement on any other basis became virtually impossible. By his stubborn attitude and refusal to negotiate with anyone except on his own terms he made sure of getting Pakistan, but also of getting it in the worst possible form — a truncated, "moth-eaten" Pakistan brought into existence by an unnatural division of the Punjab and Bengal with all the miseries that flowed therefrom. At no stage did he show signs of uneasiness at the probable consequences of his policy or seriously attempt to avert them; on the contrary, by consistently rebuffing the Sikhs, he insured that the partition of the Punjab would take place with the maximum horror. To what extent in all this he acted with his eyes open is not definitely known. Possibly in regard to the facts of the Punjab situation he deliberately preferred to remain ignorant so that knowledge might not inhibit him from the course he wished to pursue. Great achievements in action, whether divine or diabolic, require a certain ruthlessness.

It would be too uncharitable to presume — as some have done — that Jinnah, in pressing the demand for Pakistan, was actuated solely by vainglory and desire for personal power. He must have persuaded himself that some larger interests were at stake. Though not a religious man or deeply steeped in Islamic culture, he may well have genuinely believed that to safeguard the interests of the Muslims as a separate community and to preserve their distinctive character and way of life from insidious Hindu encroachment were objectives of supreme importance. Whether he was right in so believing, a non-Muslim perhaps cannot fairly judge. In any case we move into the sphere of value judgements where there are likely to be differences of opinion. Englishmen had no doubt that to escape Hitler's domination was worth a destructive war. Likewise Jinnah and his Muslim associates might maintain that to save their community from Hindu domination was worth the miseries of Partition.

But was Partition really necessary in order to secure the objectives which he had in view? It is here that the correctness, perhaps even the integrity, of his judgement may be questioned. He was right, no doubt, in distrusting Hindu professions. They may say that Muslims were their brothers, but would in fact treat them as less than stepbrothers. A few leaders might be sincere in their intentions, but the ingrained exclusiveness of the high-caste Hindus was bound to assert itself so that at most, only a few hand-picked Muslims would be embraced as brothers and the rest relegated to the position of outcastes. An excellent illustration of what treatment Muslims might expect from the Hindus, if the latter had a free choice, was afforded in the Punjab. In that province most of the commercial, industrial and banking establishments were controlled by Hindus. In none of them was any Muslim employed except in a menial capacity as a coolie or watchman or as an artisan. Well-paid posts and positions of profit were not open to outsiders, but were filled on the basis of family, caste and other similar connections according to the deeply-imbedded habits and traditions of Hindu society. That society was not go-

ing to change overnight at the pious wish of a Gandhi or a Nehru. Hindu professions were widely different from Hindu practice, as all Muslims knew. Jinnah's distrust of them was both genuine and well-founded. But it does not follow that he was right in thinking that the creation of Pakistan was necessary in order to safeguard Muslim interests. Many staunch Muslims, who shared his distrust of the Hindus and had Muslim interests at heart no less than he, were far from convinced that these could only be secured by the division of India into two separate National States. Since Muslims were in a majority in several large provinces, it was felt that, with provincial autonomy and constitutional safeguards at the Centre, they would become too powerful an element in the Indian Union for the crafty Hindus to override or circumvent their interests, however much they might desire to do so. Thus in the opinion of these Muslims — and in 1940 they were certainly a majority — the creation of Pakistan in the sense of a separate National State was unnecessary.

On the purely political plane — and in the long run this might have been all that mattered — they were probably right. Probably, too, in 1940 Jinnah himself recognized that they were right and did not intend to press the demand for Pakistan to the extreme limit. But later the tide of events which he had himself set going, reinforced by his own and his associates' personal ambitions, persuaded him that he could accept nothing less than Pakistan, even though all he could get was the husk without the kernel and at a cost in human suffering which he had not initially foreseen.

Whatever judgment may be passed on Jinnah by the moralists, he must ever be venerated by Pakistanis as the man to whom their State owes its very existence. Nor can outsiders withhold admiration. To have transformed in little more than seven years the chimerical idea of Pakistan into a living political reality was an astonishing achievement. Alike in his tenacity of purpose and in his calm, cold acceptance of consequences which would have deeply troubled the conscience of an ordinary man he showed qualities of greatness.

Gandhi's responsibility, though less direct and less deliberate than Jinnah's, was nevertheless very considerable. He did not, like Jinnah, wittingly follow a policy calculated to lead to bloodshed, but unwittingly . . . he contributed in many ways to this outcome. Moreover, as many of his utterances made clear, in pursuit of the cherished goal of Independence he was prepared, despite his proclaimed dislike of violence, to risk both bloodshed and anarchy, albeit with more reluctance and self-questioning than Jinnah.

The mistakes made by Congress under Gandhi's leadership were due basically to the Gandhian facility for self-deception. Over-conscious of his own good intentions, he clung till too late to the fallacy that Congress could and did represent all Indians including the Muslims. Obsessed by the supposedly evil intentions of the British and unaware that his own methods of appeal were calculated to provoke Muslim antipathy he shut his eyes till too late to the menace of Muslim separatism. It was easy to blame everything on the British and to persuade oneself that with their departure Hindus and Muslims would embrace as brothers. It was easy to decry the League leaders as relics of an outworn feudalism and to believe that owing to the primacy of the economic motive — one of Nehru's pet doctrines which was to be abundantly disproved — the Muslim masses would disown them. With these consoling beliefs Gandhi allowed himself to be deceived. They did not accord with facts, but they obviated the need for facing them, until at last the facts themselves confronted him in all their starkness, leaving no room for escape from partition, massacres and migrations.

There was no one to whom this outcome gave more grief than Gandhi himself. The independence for which he had striven so long seemed hardly worth having when these were its first fruits. The extent of his own responsibility for them he may not have recognized, but at least it can be said of him that he made heroic efforts to atone for his mistakes. The closing months of his life showed his character at its noblest. Unbroken in spirit by the shocks to his own hopes and ideals, he laboured to combat the frenzy that had been aroused with a sincerity and courage which cost him his life but entitled him to be looked upon as a saint and a martyr. Gandhi, indeed, may be classed with those Christian saints of the dark and middle ages who combined astute political manoeuvring (and a certain amount of humbug) with genuine moral earnestness and a courage sustained by more than mundane convictions.

Summing Up: An Indian Viewpoint

V. P. MENON

One of the most important participants in the drama of Partition was V. P. Menon, who from 1942 to 1947 was Constitutional Adviser to the Governor-General. As Mountbatten's principal adviser on constitutional matters, he played a leading part in the plan for Partition that was finally agreed upon by the Congress and League. After Independence, he worked under Sardar Patel, the Deputy Prime Minister, in the delicate task of bringing the former Indian states into the Indian Union. Menon is the author of two important works, *The Story of the Integration of the Indian States* (1956) and *The Transfer of Power* (1957), from which the following selection is taken. Menon's view of events is colored both by his involvement as an agent of the Government of India and as an Indian patriot.

DESTINY seems to have linked the course of Indo-British relations with the month of August. It was in August 1765 that Emperor Shah Alam II formally granted the *Dewani* of Bengal, Bihar and Orissa to the East India Company. In August 1858 was passed the "Act for the Better Government of India," when British India was placed under the direct government of the Crown. August 1917 will be remembered for its famous announcement, when the British Government for the first time declared the goal of their policy in India to be responsible government. It was in August 1947 that the British handed over power and left the country. The manner both of their coming and of their going was unique. They came to trade, but stayed to rule. They left of their own will; there was no war, there was no treaty — an act with no parallel in history.

The main factor responsible for the early transfer of power was the return of the Labour Party with an absolute majority in 1945. Almost the first thing they did on assuming office was to set about finding a solution of the Indian problem, a solution that would be acceptable to the two main political parties in the country, namely the Congress and the Muslim League. When they found that the parties were unable to come to any agreement, they themselves produced a plan. This was the Cabinet Mission plan, to which the Congress and the Muslim League at first reacted favourably, but on which subsequently they disagreed fundamentally on points of interpretation. The Labour Government then tried the expedient of bringing the leaders of the two parties inside an interim Government, in the hope that by working together they might come to an understanding on the long-term plan. But now the position became much worse; in coming into a common Government the leaders merely brought their outside differences inside the Cabinet. The Government of India was a house divided against itself, and the communal situation, instead of getting better, deteriorated to a state bordering

Reprinted from *The Transfer of Power* by V. P. Menon, pp. 436–440, 442, by permission of Princeton University Press. Copyright © 1957 by Princeton University Press.

99

on civil war. The Labour Government decided that the only way to redeem their pledge, while making the leaders face the grave realities of the situation, was to announce that the British would hand over power and would quit India by a definite date. The Labour Government's action was described in Parliament as a gamble and a betrayal. But let me quote the words of Sir Austen Chamberlain on another famous occasion:

Now and again in the affairs of men there comes a moment when courage is safer than prudence, when some great act of faith, touching the hearts and stirring the emotions of men, achieves a miracle that no art of statesmanship can compass.

The British Government's decision to quit India not only touched the hearts and stirred the emotions of Indians; it produced an immediate reassuring effect on the whole of South-East Asia and earned for Britain, as at no other time, universal respect and goodwill.

Though through the centuries many attempts had been made to bring India under one central Government, it was the proud claim of the British that it was they who for the first time created an Indian Empire, extending from Kashmir in the north to Cape Comorin in the south, and from Baluchistan in the west to Assam in the east. It is a sad reflection that the British who achieved that unity could not bequeath it to their successors. But sadder still is the thought that Jinnah, the hero of my generation, a great nationalist in his time and one who fought many a battle for the freedom of his country, should later have fought so successfully against its freedom, and should eventually, almost single-handed, have brought about its division.

I have indicated how Jinnah took over the Muslim League, which was then moribund, and in a few years made it the most powerful Muslim organization. When the Congress ministries resigned from the provinces and withdrew their support from the

war effort, Lord Linlithgow inevitably leaned upon the Muslims. The League grew rapidly in the sunshine of favour. It consolidated its position and soon reached the stage of asserting that the Muslims were a nation and demanding separation from the rest of India of all the provinces in which they were a majority. It was at this stage that the British Government, in their declaration of 1942, gave the right to the provinces to accede or not to accede to the Union and even to form a separate Union or Unions. This was a radical departure from the policy hitherto adopted. In the discussions leading up to the passing of the Government of India Act of 1935, it had never been contemplated that the accession of the British-Indian provinces to the Federation should be optional.

This was really the death-blow to Indian unity, and subsequent assertions of their preference for a united India by British authorities carried no weight. It was definitely a victory for Jinnah. Hereafter he could afford to stand on this declaration. When it was made in 1942, the Pakistan resolution was only two years old, and the League position, even in the Muslim-majority areas, was none too strong. But in spite of that, His Majesty's Government conceded the substance of Jinnah's demand; and this attitude persisted in all the subsequent negotiations.

When, in 1942, Sir Stafford Cripps announced His Majesty's Government's policy, the opinion was widely expressed that the British were bent upon the division of the country; that they wanted to create a Middle Eastern sphere of influence, and in pursuance of that policy wished to bring about the creation of a separate Pakistan. This would accord with their traditional liking for Muslims, with their policy of protecting the Straits and the Suez Canal from Russian influence, and with their new but overwhelming interest in the oil of Iran, Iraq and Arabia.

On the other hand, by surrendering its position of vantage and resigning its ministries in eight provinces out of the eleven, the Congress left the field entirely to the Muslim League and to the Government. If it had not resigned, it could have insisted on and got an immediate change at the Centre, especially after Japan joined the war. His Majesty's Government would not have taken the drastic step of dismissing the Congress ministries from office. Moreover, the Congress opposition to the war effort and the League's *de facto* support for it convinced the British that the Hindus generally were their enemies and the Muslims their friends, and this consideration must have added force to the silent but effective official support for the policy of partition.

Gandhiji's original instinct was sound. He stood for unconditional co-operation in the war. He was not supported by his own party, and Government was unhelpful in meeting his immediate demands. Eventually, when he found no way out and Jinnah's demand grew insistent, Gandhiji conceded self-determination for Muslim-majority areas, insisting only that there should be a central authority for the administration of certain essential subjects common to both the States. But Jinnah rejected this proposal.

When the Cabinet Mission arrived in 1946 they were thus confronted with the League's demand for a province-wise Pakistan and the Congress refusal to concede any more than a truncated Pakistan consisting merely of Muslim-majority areas.

The Cabinet Mission attempted to preserve a united India. But it was no more than a facade of unity. If their plan had worked, it would have resulted in the Muslim League securing, in substance, a province-wise Pakistan. In any case, the three-tier constitution was so unwieldy and carried with it so much potentiality for friction that it could never have been worked. Moreover, the whole structure was vitiated by an inherent instability, in that any provincial Assembly could call for a reconsideration of the terms of the constitution "after an initial period of ten years and at ten yearly intervals thereafter."

When the Labour Government found that no agreement between the parties was possible, either in the working of the interim Government or of the Constituent Assembly, on the basis of the Cabinet Mission plan, it made the bold decision that the British would quit India by a specified date. The League by this time had raised communal consciousness to such a pitch that a united India by peaceful agreement was no longer possible. The Muslim masses were behind the League; in fact, they supported the League more solidly where they were in a minority than in the Muslim-majority provinces. Even the safeguards and protection demanded for their community by the Nationalist Muslims went so far that, if acceded to, they would have prevented for all time the growth of a united nation.

In India, the province which more than any other held the key to the problem of partition was the Punjab. Official opinion in the province was divided, but Sir Bertrand Glancy, who was the Governor of the province up to 1946, was a strong advocate of a united Punjab; and his successor, Sir Evan Jenkins, who was Governor at the time of the partition, was no less so. If anyone knew the Punjab, it was surely Sir Evan Jenkins. Moreover, not all the Muslim leaders were for partition. Khizr Hyat Khan, the premier of the Punjab and leader of the Unionist Party, put up a fight in the earlier stages, but succumbed to pressure later. It has been alleged that, while he had ample resources to fight the election in 1946, he failed to use them. It is possible that if he had been given sufficient official encouragement, he would have fought against the disintegration of the province. But when, owing to his resignation, the Unionist Party was dissolved, the fate of the Punjab was sealed.

When Lord Mountbatten arrived on the scene, he soon realised that the Cabinet Mission plan was unacceptable to the parties, and some form of partition was inevitable. He prepared a plan, the basis of which was demission of power to the provinces, or to such confederations as the provinces might decide to form before the transfer of power. The responsibility for partition was left to the popular choice. When this plan was shown to Nehru he reacted strongly against it. Thereupon Lord Mountbatten fell back on the alternative plan of two Dominions, of which Pakistan would comprise the Muslim-majority areas only. The Congress agreed to this, and by accepting Dominion Status removed one of the great obstacles which had hitherto stood between them and the British. Thereafter the League was no longer able to derive advantage from the fact that it had agreed to remain within the Commonwealth while the Congress claimed complete independence. Thenceforth things moved smoothly, and in every step that Lord Mountbatten took he carried the support of the party leaders. . . .

Pakistan today is an Islamic State. There is no minority problem in West Pakistan, while East Pakistan is being steadily drained of its Hindus. India on the other hand still has a population of about forty million Muslims, besides other minorities, to protect and care for. Gandhiji particularly emphasized that the minorities were a sacred trust in the hands of the majority. It was a cause most dear to his heart. He lived for it — indeed he eventually died for it! India will surely be true to his precepts. I have no doubt that, despite the heavy strain which the policy of Pakistan imposes on the Government of India, the latter will steadfastly maintain and fulfil its great ideal of a truly secular State.

That the future of the two countries depends upon mutual good relations is almost a truism. The partition of August 1947 was surely not intended to sunder for all time the ties that for a century and a half have bound India together as one administrative, political and economic unit. Geographically and economically at least, those ties persist in spite of the partition and the serious effect which its aftermath has had upon the economy of the Punjab and Bengal. The prosperity of the Punjab was due to the sweat and toil of irrigation engineers. There is no reason why East and West Punjab should not continue to enjoy the fruits of those labours by mutual give and take. Similarly, the economy of West Bengal is inextricably tied up with that of East Bengal, and vice versa. Neither side can afford to ignore the circumstances of geography and the economic interests which draw them together. Economically it is the common man who must suffer, but the suffering of the common man can surely be assuaged on both sides by the healing touch of good neighbourliness. It is never too late for men of goodwill to take stock of realities, for the leaders to sit down calmly and dispassionately, and together evolve some common machinery which would not merely minimize the rigours of partition but, by banishing all sense of fear and conflict, would bring about for both countries enduring peace and progress.

SUGGESTIONS FOR ADDITIONAL READING

Literature dealing with the partition of India is growing but, as yet, there are few special studies bearing exclusively on this momentous historical event. Two of the most important are: Khalid Bin Sayeed, *Pakistan, the Formative Phase* (Karachi: 1960), and Penderel Moon, *Divide and Quit* (Berkeley: 1961). An excellent account of the dramatic events from 1945 to 1947 preceding partition is given in E. W. R. Lumby, *The Transfer of Power in India* (London, 1954). In a class by itself is V. P. Menon's *The Transfer of Power* (Princeton, 1957), a definitive study of the historical background and the immediate events leading to partition. General histories providing useful material on partition and its antecedents are: Percival Spear, *India: A Modern History* (Ann Arbor: 1961); Vincent A. Smith, *The Oxford History of India* (Oxford: 1958, 3rd edition); and T. Walter Wallbank, *India in the New Era* (Chicago: 1951) and a revised and abridged edition, *A Short History of India and Pakistan* (New York: 1965, 2nd edition). Sir Percival Griffiths in his *The British Impact on India* (London: 1952) gives a solid treatment of the rise of Indian nationalism and its relationship to the emergence of a Muslim national movement and separatism. Brief but useful accounts may be found in Ian Stephens, *Pakistan* (London: 1964); J. B. Das Gupta, *Indo-Pakistan Relations* (Amsterdam: 1960); L. F. Rushbrook Williams, *The State of Pakistan* (London: 1962); and Keith Callard's "Pakistan," in George M. Kahin, *Major Governments of Asia* (Ithica: 1961). Edward Thompson and G. T. Garratt present an excellent history of the development of nationalism and communal relations from the advent of the Europeans to the 1930's in their *Rise and Fulfillment of British Rule in India* (London, 1934). William Roy Smith's *Nationalism and Reform in India* (New Haven, 1938) describes and evaluates the political developments from the end of World War I to the Government of India Act of 1935, giving special emphasis to Hindu-Muslim relations. *The Indian Problem* (New York: 1944) by Sir Reginald Coupland is a scholarly analysis of pertinent issues as seen in the closing phase of World War I. While by no means definitive, Hector Bolitho's biography *Jinnah: Creator of Pakistan* (London: 1954) will be found useful. S. M. Ikram's *Muslim Civilization* (edited by Ainslie T. Embree, New York, 1964) is excellent for the Muslim period, especially the interaction between Islam and Hinduism. The following are vivid accounts of personalities and events by eyewitnesses of partition: Robert Aura Smith, *Divided India* (New York: 1947); George E. Jones, *Tumult in India* (New York: 1948); and Sir Francis Tuker, *While Memory Serves* (London: 1950). Margaret Bourke-White's *Halfway to Freedom* (New York: 1949) is notable for its graphic pictures portraying the violent aftermath of partition. An interesting artistic recreation of conditions in India on the eve of partition may be found in John Masters' novel, *Bhowani Junction* (New York, 1954). Pertinent documents are given in C. H. Philips, *The Evolution of India and Pakistan* (London, 1962), and Sir Maurice Gwyer and A. Appadorai, *Speeches and Documents on the Indian Constitution* (New York. 1957).